PARENTS & KIDS TOGETHER

Lisa Lyons Durkin

Together Activities
and Additional
Material by
Kathy Faggella

WARNER BOOKS

A Warner Communications Company

Copyright © 1986 by Lisa Lyons Durkin

The following pages are reprinted from *Crayons, Crafts and Concepts* by Kathy Faggella by permission of First Teacher, Inc.: 29, 37, 88, 95, 123, 127, 141.
The following pages are reprinted from *Concept Cookery* by Kathy Faggella by permission of First Teacher, Inc.: 61, 62, 63, 65, 66, 71, 69, 72, 73, 74, 75, 76, 77, 129, 169.

Bug Keeper and Net on page 101 reprinted with permission from
TEACHABLES FROM TRASHABLES
Copyright 1979, Toys 'N Things Press, a division of
Resources for Childcaring, Inc.
906 N. Dale St.
St. Paul, MN 55103

A Warner Communications Company
Warner Books, Inc., 666 Fifth Avenue, New York, NY 10103

Design by Alice Cooke, A to Z Design, NYC

Cover Design by Alice Cooke; Illustration by Debby Dixler

Copyediting and skills charts by Martha A. Hayes

Art by Debby Dixler

Printed in the United States of America

First Printing: May 1986

10 9 8 7 6 5 4 3 2 1

Library of Congress Cataloging-in-Publication Data

Durkin, Lisa Lyons.
   Parents & kids together.

   1. Play. 2. Creative activities and seat work.
3. Child development. 4. Parent and child. I. Title.
II. Title: Parents and kids together.
HQ782.D87 1986   649'.511   85-29488
ISBN 0-446-37014-2 (U.S.A.) (pbk.)
      0-446-37017-7 (Canada) (pbk.)

ACKNOWLEDGMENTS

I would like to gratefully acknowledge the contributions of everyone who has written articles for *First Teacher* over the past seven years. Their contributions have helped to create the *First Teacher* philosophy and to make this book possible. Most especially, I would like to thank Debby Dixler and Dr. Bena Kallick who first brought me the Early Childhood materials and helped to give birth to *First Teacher*, and all the people at the Teachers' Center at Fairfield who were such an important part of its infancy.

I wish also to acknowledge the specific articles in *First Teacher* from which I researched the ideas for *Parents and Kids, Together.*

Chapter 1: "How the Child Develops" by Ellen Goldstein (April, 1981); "In the Sea of Learning" by Dr. Lydia A. Duggins (Sept., 1982); "It Makes Good Sense" by Martha A. Hayes (Oct., 1982) "Learning Through Toys: It's Child's Play" by Harriet Miller Ettenson (Nov., 1982); "Popping the Question" by Mary Jo Puckett Cliat and Jean M. Shaw (Aug., 1981); "Quality, Not Quantity" by Gena Rotas (Nov., 1980); "Stages of Play" by Dr. Sally Bing (Feb., 1984); "Starters" by Janet Horowitz (Dec., 1981); "Success-filled Kids" by Dr. Billie Joan Thomas (Feb., 1982); "The Magic of Thinking" by Martha A. Hayes (Sept., 1982); "When Kids Develop Independence" by Janet Horowitz (July, 1982).

Chapter 2: "A Bedtime Story" by Ellen Schmidt (April, 1980); "Alligators and Submarines" by Ellen Javernick (July/Aug., 1985); "Bathe and Learn" by Janet Horowitz (July, 1980); "Calendars for Kids" by Janet Horowitz (Mar., 1982); "Cozy Places and Organized Spaces" by Janet Horowitz and Dr. Anne H. Leone (April, 1983); "From Home to School" by Sherry Burrell (Aug., 1984); "Getting Past the Mess" by Ellen Schmidt (July, 1980); "How Many Sleeps Until. . ." by Dr. Rosalind Charlesworth (Mar., 1982); "How to Begin a Day" by Ellen Schmidt (Preview issue); "In the Book Corner" by Dr. Rosalind Charlesworth (Mar., 1982); "Kids' Dressing" by Karen Marlow (July, 1982); "Learning Time Takes Time" by Dr. Anne S. Peskin (Mar., 1982); "Making Mealtimes Happy Times" by Sherry Burrell (Nov., 1983); "Pack Up Your Routines" by Dr. Billie Joan Thomas (June, 1983); "Practice Makes Better" by Carol Keepler (July, 1982); "See You Later, Alligator" by Bobbi Katz (Mar., 1982); "Simple Science with Water" by Kathy Faggella and Alice Kelly (July, 1980); "Taking the Sting Out of Goodbye" by Nancy McKeever (Preview issue); "The Water Table" by Ellen Goldstein (July, 1980); "Time to Teach Time" by Dr. Lydia A. Duggins (Mar., 1982); "To Dream or Not to Dream" by Janet S. Brown (May, 1982); "Toys, Toys, Everywhere" by Fretta Reitzes (Nov., 1980); "Water Babies" by Dr. Anne H. Leone (May, 1983); "What's in a Name?" by Janet Horowitz (Sept., 1983); "Which Comes First?" by Martha A. Hayes (Mar., 1982); "You, Your Child, and Water" by Janet Horowitz (July, 1980).

Chapter 3: "Create Math Games and Toys" by Sherry Burrell (Sept., 1981); "Discover Water" by Kathleen Koons (July/Aug., 1985); "Feelin' Good about Math" by Dr. Bernard R. Yvon (Sept., 1982); "Language Around the House" by Sandra Gratias (Oct., 1982); "Laughing with Words" by Kathy Faggella and Janet Horowitz (Oct., 1982); "Master Math with Materials" by Nancy McKeever (Sept., 1981); "Play Learning" by Renee Wittenberg (Oct., 1982); "Shadows, Bubbles, and Balloons" by Dr. Margery A. Kranyik (Sept., 1982); "Talking Games by Susan Coons (Feb., 1984).

Chapter 4: "Create Math Games and Toys" by Sherry Burrell (Sept., 1981); "Eat, Drink, and Be Merry" by Dr. Margery A. Kranyik (Nov., 1983); "Hot and Cold" by Martha A. Hayes (Nov., 1983); "In the Book Corner" by Mary Underhill (Nov., 1983); "In the Kitchen" by Martha A. Hayes (Nov., 1983); "Let's Get Physical" by Jean Stangl (Nov., 1983); "Math at Home" by Harriet Miller Ettenson (Sept., 1981); "Preschoolers Can Be Kitchen Helpers" by Gena Rotas and Alice Kelly (April, 1980); "The First Teacher Guide to Snacking" by Janet Horowitz (April, 1980).

Chapter 5: "Alligators and Submarines" by Ellen Javernick (July/Aug., 1985); "Build a Homemade Ant Farm" by Beth Schapira (April, 1983); "Explore Your Own Backyard" by Jean Stangl (April, 1983); "Plants to Grow With" by Jean Stangl (June, 1985); "Shadows, Bubbles, and Balloons" by Dr. Margery A. Kranyik (Sept., 1983); "Small Animals, Big Discoveries" by Janet Horowitz (May, 1982); "The Tree of Life" by Janet Horowtz (Oct., 1983); "We All Begin in the Fall" by Karel Kilimnik (Sept., 1985); "Whatever Happened to Mud Pies?" by Jean Stagnl (July/Aug., 1985).

Chapter 6: "Action in Small Spaces" by Dr. Billie Joan Thomas (May, 1983); "A Trip to a Department Store" by Kathy Faggella and Alice Kelly (Preview issue); "A Trip to the Library" by Ellen Goldstein (Feb., 1980); "Falling in Love with a Book" by Dr. Lydia A. Duggins (Nov., 1984); "Money and Your Child" by Janet Horowitz (Sept., 1980); "Strangers: Important Lessons" by Dr. Sally Bing (Dec., 1984); "When Your Child Visits You at Work" by Janet Horowtz (Jan., 1983).

Chapter 7: "Just Around the Corner" by Dr. Billie Joan Thomas (April, 1984); "On the Road to Reading: Play Games to Pass the Time" by Gena Rotas (Aug., 1981); "Over the River. . ." by Martha A. Hayes (June, 1983); "Pack a Little Music" by Mary Ann Hall (June, 1983); "Rainy Day Fun" by Mary Jo Puckett Cliat and Jean M. Shaw (Mar., 1982); "Take Your Senses for a Walk" by Kathleen Allan Meyer (Sept., 1982); "Travel Activity Kit" by Kathy Faggella and Janet Horowitz (June, 1981).

Chapter 8: "Be Honest: Why Is the TV On?" by Gena Rotas (Jan., 1981); "Books Are Bridges" by Dr. Anne H. Leone (Aug., 1984); "Card and Chalk Games" by Janet Horowitz (Feb., 1984); "Doing Your Own Thing with Your Child" by Felicial Baker (Nov., 1980); "Games for Thinking" by Martha A. Hayes (Feb., 1984); "Getting the Most Out of TV: Making Choices" by Janet Horowitz (July, 1982); "Helping Kids Cope with TV Commercials" by Janet Horowitz (Sept., 1982); "In the Book Corner" by Janet Horowitz (Sept., 1984); "Is TV a Learning Tool for the Young Child?" by Nancy McKeever (Jan., 1981); "Make a Bookworm" by Dr. Lydia A. Duggins (Aug., 1981); "Over, Under, In and Out" by Stella Dennis (Aug., 1982); "Preschool Carpenters" by Jean Stangl (April, 1984); "Rare Books" by Mary Beth Spann Cicio (Nov., 1981); "Ready, Set, Read" by Janet Horowitz (Aug., 1981); "Stories as Stepping Stones" by Phyllis Halloran (Nov., 1981); "The Joy of Reading" by Phillis Halloran (Aug., 1981); "To Watch or Not to Watch: Is That the Question?" by Harriet Miller Ettenson (Jan., 1981); "TV Tech" by Beth Schapira (Mar., 1983); "Wood Works Wonders" by Fran DeMaria (Aug., 1982).

Chapter 9: "Before Sports" by Martha A. Hayes (May, 1983); "Brains and Brawn" by Dr. Billie Joan Thomas (July, 1982); "Exercise DOS and DON'TS" by Jean Stangl (April, 1985); "If Your Family Is Batty About Baseball" by Janet Horowitz (May, 1983); "Inner Winners" by Sherry Burrell (May, 1983); "When Everyone Is Watching Football on TV" by Janet Horowitz (Nov., 1982); "Yoga for Kids" by Sherry Burrell (Dec., 1981).

Chapter 10: "Celebrations: Big and Small" by Sherry Burrell (Oct., 1980); "Games and Songs for Parties" by Janet Horowitz (Feb., 1984); "Getting to Know You" by Janet Horowitz (Dec., 1982); "Guess Who's Coming to Visit?" by Sandra Gratias (Dec., 1984); "Helpful Holiday Hints" by Carol Keepler (Nov., 1982); "Holiday Visits Made Easy" by Janet Horowitz (Nov., 1982); "Make Parties for Pre-schoolers Fun and Easy" by Janet Horowitz (Oct., 1984); "That New Baby" by Ellen K. Hasbrouck (Dec., 1984).

My special thanks to Phyllis Halloran and Dr. Anne H. Leone, whose "In the Book Corner" columns make looking for books to suggest in *Parents and Kids Together* so easy and delightful.

TABLE OF

CONTENTS

ACTIVITIES AND RECIPES TO DO TOGETHER

To my PARENTS,
who encouraged me.

To the KIDS—
Jennifer, Christopher, Patrick, and Michael—
who inspired me.

To my husband,
who makes everything work TOGETHER.

Foreword

I am writing this book for myself as much as for you, my readers. Like most of you, I am the parent of a young child. Like many of you, I am a working parent. Unlike most of you, I am fortunate in that my work brings me in contact with many ideas and activities for young children through informative articles. I am the editor of <u>First Teacher</u>, a monthly newspaper for teachers of toddlers and preschoolers. For seven years, my job has been to edit articles for these age groups full of practical advice and wonderful projects, games, and recipes. But when it comes to finding that perfect learning activity for my child and me to do together, I am often at a loss. For one thing, my day is not organized like that of the preschool teachers to whom <u>First Teacher</u> is addressed; I have to do cleaning, cooking, gardening, errands, shopping, and, of course, my work. At the same time, I want to provide a stimulating learning environment for my child. For another, I am not a trained Early Childhood professional with years of experience to give me ideas and often moral support.

However, after editing almost 100 issues of <u>First Teacher</u>, I have learned two very important, but basic, facts about young children.
■ Eighty percent of a person's lifetime learning takes place in the first six years.
■ All of a child's early experiences are learning experiences, affecting his social, emotional, intellectual, and physical growth.

So, parents provide those important first learning experiences that enable their child to develop into a happy, healthy, independent individual. They are truly their child's "first teacher."

"But, I am NOT a teacher," you protest. "My child learns (or will learn) in school," you insist. "I am a busy person, as well as a loving, concerned parent," you explain. These are the reasons why I have poured over those 100 issues of the newspaper and compiled the best it has to offer parents like myself. The book that follows is a wealth of learning experiences for you to share with your child or children, organized in such a way that they fit into YOUR life, the things you have to do, and the things you enjoy.

The most valuable experiences you share with your child are the ones when you are relaxed and having a good time. Some of the experiences I have chosen to share are simple two-line word games to be played when you are doing the laundry, raking leaves, or driving to the store. Others take some time and preparation on your part and your total attention while you and your child are doing them. They should be scheduled into "quality time"—time you have put aside to do a special project together. (That time, because of a young child's short attention span, is more likely to be half an hour than a whole afternoon.) Some of the experiences will delight both of you or perhaps the whole family, and you will want to tuck them in your treasure chest of things to do over and over. You will find many, many times to use these experiences, to add to them, or to change them to suit the season or special occasion. Others, you and your child will find are "yucky" and don't work for either of you. Still others will appeal to one of you, and because you are both individuals with your own likes and dislikes, and your own styles of learning, someone will have to make compromises (a valuable learning experience in itself).

TOGETHER activities are placed in special parts of the book because they fit in naturally with certain experiences. They are meant, however, to be used whenever you and your child have a large amount of time to spend together and you are looking for a specific activity. They are especially useful when you have been forced to say to your child "*Not now,*" when he asks you to play. Turn a disappointing answer into an invitation for fun by adding "*Go look in our special book and pick out an activity for us to do together after I finish the laundry (or this afternoon, or tomorrow morning after breakfast).*"

Doing the **TOGETHER** activities can be enriching and fun as long as everyone involved wants to be there. When your mind isn't on play (but on your job or dinner), it's not the time for this kind of shared experience. Treat this time like a very special appointment. During these special moments, your child has your TOTAL, UNDIVIDED ATTENTION. He knows you think he is special and that makes him feel special about himself.

Every suggestion in this book has been child-tested and recommended by preschool teachers and Early Childhood professionals. They are also recommended by me, a loving, but busy, parent of a preschooler, who wants to use every possible opportunity to help my child grow into a happy, healthy, independent individual.

INTRODUCTION 1

Your child's first teacher

Play-filled lessons

Basic concepts everywhere

A question of questions

Tips for first teachers

A little declaration of

independence

Teacher, guide, observer

Your Child's First Teacher

You are your child's first teacher. Does that statement scare you? It shouldn't. If you feel uncomfortable with the term "teacher," substitute "guide." If your child is anything like mine, he is more of an explorer than a student anyway.

Dr. Jean Piaget, upon whose theories the foundations of Early Childhood education have been built, said just that—the young child is an explorer and it is the job of the adults around him to provide the experiences and materials to stimulate his development.

Very briefly, Piaget found that children go through different stages of development. In the first stage, from birth to eighteen months, the child begins actively to take part in his own learning without any real understanding of what is happening. At first, the child believes that things exist only if they can be seen, heard, or touched. The youngest child thinks very differently from older children and adults. His idea of the world is full of misunderstandings.

In the second stage, from eighteen months to seven years, the child begins to separate himself from the world around him. He begins to show that he thinks about things before doing them. This is the time when the child often has a hard time separating fantasy from reality. *"Is Kermit, the frog, real?"* he says.

Piaget saw the tremendous importance of play during this stage. When we give a child the opportunity to play, experiment, talk, and enjoy his surroundings, we are helping him learn more about the world, other people, and himself.

1. BIRTH-18 MONTHS: EXPLORATION — "Look at the water splash!"

2. 18 MONTHS-7 YEARS: BEGINNING LANGUAGE — "I want yours- it has more water."

3. 7-12 YEARS: WORKS WITH MATERIALS

4. 12 YEARS+ ABSTRACT THINKING — "A WORD PROBLEM: If a container of water holds 1 cup, then, how many..."

Play-Filled Lessons

Just as you are your child's "first teacher," play activities make up his first lessons. Play is a child's work. His first job is to learn how to get along in the world—and he does this through play. By encouraging his play and exposing him to new experiences, you are being a first-rate "teacher." Part of your teaching job is to know and make available the toys, games, materials, and "playful" experiences that are right for your child.

puppets

A baby is interested in watching, tasting, and touching everything in the strange and wonderful world around him. Thus, his first playthings are his senses. The toddler is mainly interested in getting around and using his body to learn and do new and interesting things. Objects from the "real world" are very important to the toddler. Pots and pans, telephones, pocketbooks, umbrellas, and gardening tools give the toddler a sense of self-confidence because he can use the things he sees grown-ups using.

The preschooler has developed a good idea of how the world works, how to get his body to do what he wants, and how to get along with others. He practices his newly learned skills through play. He doesn't require a lot of toys, but he needs a variety of very structured, semi-structured, and open-ended toys and materials to practice his skills and to express his ideas and feelings. Games, books, and tricycles help your child to master skills. Less structured materials, like blocks, balls, and a large scarf, help him use his imagination and add his own ideas to the play. Unstructured play materials like paints, clay, and water allow the freest expression of all. These materials often allow children to express their feelings in a concrete way. Thoughts and ideas can take shape and almost become real when constructed by your child using a play material. He can be a sailor in the bathtub or a chef creating a gourmet meal out of play dough. He can draw that monster under his bed with crayons and then tear it up, along with some of his fear.

You need to keep a balance of these toys and play materials around the house. After all, your home is your child's first classroom.

scarves

OPEN-ENDED OR LEAST STRUCTURED PLAY MATERIALS

PAINT- with brushes or hands

WATER

CLAY

SAND

Basic Concepts Everywhere

You have endless opportunities to help your child learn. Just look around you—there are basic concepts everywhere. That is what this book is all about.

Your home is your child's first classroom; and every time you go out with your child, you are taking a field trip full of marvelous opportunities.

Just like the preschool teacher, your job is to introduce and reinforce the concepts over and over again through daily routines and everyday experiences. Let your child experience numbers as you count balloons at the zoo or look at the license plate on your car. Let him practice one-to-one correspondence as he sets the table with one plate, one fork, and one spoon in front of each chair. Talk about colors when you make bubbles with dishwashing liquid and help your child experiment with things that sink and float in the bathtub. Let your child taste a sweet pickle and then a sour one. Through these experiences, you are helping prepare him for the concepts he will be "learning" in school.

Putting on socks before shoes.

Your child needs to develop thinking skills, as well as basic concepts, in his early years; many of these will require him to find out or figure out by reasoning. In reading, this inferential thinking skill is often called *"reading between the lines."*

Using water when told to wash hands.

Your child will develop this kind of thinking through the many and different kinds of experiences you provide. By presenting him with new situations, and relating new events to familiar ones, you are helping him better understand and face them in a more mature way.

Turning doorknob so that door can be pulled open.

You can help your child develop his thinking skills through frequent discussions. At first, just the naming of objects and the description of actions add to your child's understanding of experiences. Then, if you talk about the "whys," he also learns about cause and effect—that there are reasons for each event that occurs. Soon, he will realize that often the causes are not discussed and he must figure them out for himself.

A question of questions

There is an art to having discussions with your child. The questions you ask during them are very important. Avoid questions that call for only *yes* or *no* answers because these require no real thought from your child, and they often can end a discussion.

Inserting letter in mailbox in order for message to be delivered.

Ask some questions that call for one good answer— *"How old are you?"* This type of question helps your child learn new vocabulary words and how to classify.

Still other types of questions have many possible answers— *"How would you* decorate this cake?" "What do you think happened to Goldilocks after she ran away from the bears?" Questions like these stretch your child's mind because they make him explore many possibilities. He is still an explorer; now not just with his senses, however, but also with his mind. These questions encourage your child to think creatively.

Many of the activities in this book help you encourage your child's creativity, partly through the questions that can accompany them. Children develop their imagination over time by constantly imitating the things and people around them. Everything your child sees, he uses. Help him become a better observer by pointing things out. Involve your child in your activities, and explain as you do them.

Then, help him make the transition from reality to make believe with some "What ifs."

■ "What if the floor I am mopping were all water? How would you cross it?"
■ "What if you were a tree? How would you look?"
■ "If this box contained a gift, what would it be?"

One final thought on questions. Children use questions to get many results. Think about their questions as carefully as you formulate your own.

THE NON-VERBAL QUESTION

This type of question is seen through the child's gestures and facial expressions. Often the child will tug at the adult and seemingly ask, "Can you help me?"

THE PRACTICE QUESTION

With the acquisition of words and language comes the fun of repetition. A child might make this type of question into a game by asking, "What color is my shirt?" then answering, "Red." "What color are my pants?" then answering, "Blue." This question can be a game or a way of absorbing new knowledge.

THE CLASSIFICATION QUESTION

These questions help sort out data, make comparisons, and then organize information..... "Teddy is furry..... So is my dog, Spot..... Is Teddy a dog? No, Teddy is a bear."

THE INFORMATION QUESTION

Children really want to know why the sky is blue or what makes a rainbow.

THE SECURITY QUESTION

These questions grow out of fears children naturally experience: "Will Jaws fit in our swimming pool? Will you die soon?"

THE PSEUDO QUESTION

Children often use questions even when they don't really want or expect information or reassurance.

Why do I have to go to bed?

REALLY MEANS

"Can I go to bed later?"

Did you know I went to an ice skating party?

REALLY MEANS

"I'm telling you I went to an ice skating party."

Do you like my new dress?

REALLY MEANS

"I want you to notice and admire my new dress."

This question wants your interest as much as your answer.

THE HIDDEN AGENDA QUESTION

What time are you leaving my dance class?

MIGHT REALLY MEAN

"Why do you have to leave me alone? I want you to stay."

It is important for the adult to reflect the child's true feeling by saying.....

I guess you'd like to have me watch you dance for a while longer

Tips for First Teachers

Before you dive into the activities, projects, and recipes that follow, there are a few tips I would like to share, to help ensure that the upcoming learning experiences are as meaningful as possible.

▶ When you have something important to say to your preschooler, go to him and get down on his level. If you speak to him from across the room, it is likely he won't hear you or understand you.

▶ Guide through orienting rather than directing. In this way, you are teaching your child something, not just giving orders.

SAY: *"The bikes go in the shed." "The forks go on the table."*

DON'T SAY: *"Put the bikes in the shed." "Set the table."*

YES "There is 1 more block under the chair."

NOT "Get the block from under the chair."

▶ Give choices only when you mean to. For example: DON'T SAY: *"Do you want to wash your hands now?"* when your child comes in covered with mud.

▶ Try not to make value judgments when you talk to your child. Instead, talk about the effects of the child's actions so he can understand why he should change his behavior.

YES "When you pour paint on the floor it makes a mess and I don't like it. Now, let's get a sponge."

NOT "You are very bad to have done that— BAD GIRL."

▶ When you give directions, let your child know what he can do, not just what he can't do.

YES "You can throw the ball when we go outside. You can throw the BEANBAG indoors."

NOT "Don't throw the ball indoors."

▶ Talk about the activity, not the total child. When guiding behavior, be as clear as possible as to what you want.

YES = "You did such a careful job of cleaning up. You hung up the smock and washed the brushes. THANK YOU!"

NOT = "What a good boy for cleaning up."

▶ It is important that your child succeed most of the time. Sometimes, this means giving him simpler tasks; other times, it means providing more challenging ones. Try to provide activities that use your child's strengths and help him cope with his weaknesses.

Make sure that your child is aware of his successes. Everyone knows that a little praise goes a long way, but a "little praise" really needs to be more than the same few phrases repeated over and over. Your child is entitled to more than "good," "very good," or "fine," if encouragement and good self-image are your goals. Try some of the suggestions below and you'll feel as special as your child when you see the smile of satisfaction on his face.

A little declaration of independence

You want your child to be happy, healthy, and feel independent. Yours is a tough job. Not only that, it's the hardest when you think things will be getting easier—when your child begins to move toward independence.

In almost the same moment, your child will be demanding freedom and clinging to you. It takes a lot of adult time and energy to deal with the temper tantrums, whining, questions, and tugs-of-war that are part of this move, but the end result is worth it. He will be able to make decisions for himself, do things in his own way, and most important, have the self-confidence to experience all that life has to offer.

Here are some tips from educational psychologist, Janet Horowitz, on how to help your child develop independence and maintain your own sanity.

▶ Have patience. Let your child assert his independence, even though it means more work for you. Let him water the plants, even though you have to mop up the spills; let him try to dress himself, help in the kitchen, and set the table. The only way he can learn how to be independent is by being allowed to do things on his own.

▶ Let him help. Give him jobs you know he can do. Then, he won't ask to do the ones that are too difficult for him. (Give him pots and pans to dry; then he won't ask to dry your good china.)

▶ Set limits. Make it clear that there are certain things that he just cannot do—use sharp knives, touch poisonous cleaning agents, or throw his toys around. Stay FIRM on these.

▶ Give approval when a task is completed and he will feel proud. *"You did a terrific job of picking up the toys in your room."*

▶ Respect him as a person with his own likes and dislikes. Give in on unimportant battles, so that you can stand firm on health and safety rules. *"You may wear either the red or the green sweater today, but you must wear a warm one."*

Learning to make choices is a very important part of becoming independent. By giving your child choices from an early age, you are giving him practice in decision-making. Even at the age of two, allowing a child to choose between two shirts to wear or two cups to drink from makes him feel more grown-up and in control of his world.

You have many opportunities to give your child choices—choosing the last piece of equipment to play on before you go home makes leaving the playground easier; choosing between two healthy snacks can make your child forget that he originally wanted candy; choosing the story at bedtime and the person who will tuck him in can make him forget that he really didn't want to go to bed at all. All he honestly wants to know is that his opinion counts.

▶ Be flexible. Things don't have to be perfect—so what if he matched the wrong pairs of socks. Compliment him for putting on his socks by himself.

▶ Allow more time for doing things. Hurrying and nagging your child only makes things worse. (Leave an extra ten minutes for putting on galoshes to be safe.)

▶ Think prevention. Don't try and do things when your child is too tired because his demands may become impossible and unrealistic.

▶ Provide the information necessary to be successful. When your child wants to do something, make sure he knows exactly what to do, so that he can be successful. *"Put the dog food in the red bowl and the water in the white bowl."*

▶ Trust your own judgment when making decisions about how much independence to allow your child. In addition, check with other parents, teachers, and in books. There is no one right way.

▶ Allow your child to fail. It's through failure that we learn about ourselves, and what better place to fail than in our own homes or in the presence of caring adults who offer encouragement to try again.

Make use of these tips and there won't be a war following your child's declaration of independence.

Teacher, Guide, Observer

During these special times with your child, there is one more very important role you can play—that of observer. Dr. Jean Piaget, whose theories on young children and learning began this chapter, developed his ideas through many years of observation. Early Childhood teachers are trained in "observing and recording"—keeping notes on patterns, potential problems, and exciting events in the lives of the children they work with.

You needn't keep records, but your observations of your child will help you provide the right experiences, materials, and support for his steady growth and development. I won't burden you with a long list of things to look at, but there is one key set of observations you can make that can have an important effect on your child's future educational career. They relate to his own special learning style.

We all learn through our senses, especially sight, hearing, and touch; but many people, in particular younger children, rely on one of these senses more than the others to take in information and store it in their memory. In fact, according to experts, about thirty percent of elementary school children learn basically through their sense of sight; twenty-five percent rely primarily on their hearing to help their memorization of information; fifteen percent have a very strong sense of touch. The remaining thirty percent use a combination of these senses.

As they grow up, everyone learns to use all their senses to some extent, but understanding the way in which your child learns best NOW can be very important in his later learning and educational experiences. Better than anyone else, you are in a position to observe your child and discover his strengths and weaknesses—and share them with his teachers. With so many children to work with, teachers can sometimes miss your child's special learning style—and that can be disastrous. A child who learns visually will have a hard time learning to read through the phonics method. He can become frustrated and begin to feel "dumb and inferior" if he is being taught through sounds alone. He could be turned off reading for life in Kindergarten or the first grade!

Take a look at the chart on the next page. It describes the learning styles of three children—Victor is visual; Alice learns primarily through what she hears; Kathy has a very strong tactile sense. Does one of the descriptions remind you of anyone? If so, file away the information. Keep it in mind as you do the activities in this book and share it with your child's teachers at the appropriate time.

What comes next is the good stuff. The rest of the book is for you and your child—to learn together, to grow together, to enjoy together. You are your child's first teacher—and you are the best teacher he will ever have!

ROOMS AND ROUTINES 2

Organizing your space

Private places

Organizing your time

Morning routines

Getting dressed

Going to school

Time to take a bath

The bathtub scientist

The bathtub swimmer

Time to have a meal

Before the meal

During the meal

Mealtime fun and learning

Time to go to bed

Organizing Your Space

Your home is your castle; but, as I said before, it is also a classroom for your child. Whether you live in a small apartment or a large house, part of your job as a parent is to make room for all the toys and games your child uses, to find places indoors as well as outdoors for your child to play freely, AND also to leave some private, off-limits space for yourself.

In the living room, dining room, or den, provide one small storage place in a corner in which to tuck toys neatly away. Large baskets, colorful plastic boxes, or wooden boxes put on wheels hold a lot and can be hidden behind a large chair, placed in a corner, or carted into another room at the end of the day. In addition, give your child a small section of the family bookshelf for his favorites. When you read, he will be encouraged to do the same.

In the kitchen, put aside a place for his cooking toys and dishes. Keep a special box for water toys near the sink. If possible, have a section of a shelf for crayons, watercolors, play dough, and paper. All these will provide things for your child to do by himself while you are working in the kitchen. Try to have a separate space—a small table or countertop area for him to use—near you, but not in the middle of the cake batter or the peeled potatoes.

Be clear about areas where you don't want your child to play, where no toys are to be kept. Parents need their own private space where they don't see or think about their child's toys. Adults need places to get away from it all—to think, read, paint, listen to music, or do some other creative or quiet activity.

TOGETHER

Children love things that are personalized. Use one or all of the suggestions on the facing page to make your child's room really special—and personal.

Children also need to have their own special place in which to retreat—to relax, read, paint, listen to music, or just to BE. If your child has his own room, you can create a wonderful environment within that room to provide relaxation or stimulation. These special places can be just a corner, a small chest, a tiny table and chair, part of a wall, a cubby, storage box, or shelves. Here are some cozy places you can provide for your child to enjoy.

A MUSIC CORNER
Include:

■ a record player or tape recorder—sturdy ones that your child can operate himself are best.

■ records or tapes—there are wonderful ones available in many libraries. Store them someplace where they are easy for your child to reach.

■ instruments—either bought or homemade. Try making some of these. Keep them stored in a small box in easy reach.

■ scarves—to wave or dance with to music. Store in the box with the instruments.

■ a comfortable pillow or low chair to sit on.

PERSONALIZED PROJECTS

YOU'LL NEED:
wooden hanger · paint brush · t-shirt · iron—ADULT USE ONLY · permanent felt tip markers · polyester stuffing or old stockings · felt squares-in your child's favorite colors · acrylic paints · old newspaper · iron-on fabric patches or tape · needle and thread · ¼ yd. felt · glue · scissors

WHAT TO DO:

NAME HANGER

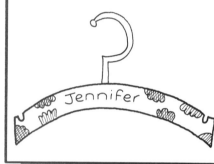

1. Spread old newspaper on the floor and put wooden hanger on it.
2. Paint your child's name on the hanger.
3. Your child paints on decorations.
4. Let hanger dry thoroughly before using.

T-SHIRT PILLOW

1. Cut out letters of your child's name from patches or tape. Your child may want to cut out some of his own shapes and designs.
2. Iron onto t-shirt, according to directions.
3. Add more designs with permanent markers. (If you don't have patches or tape, use permanent markers for name and designs.)
4. Stuff t-shirt with polyester stuffing or old stockings and sew at bottom, neck, and sleeves.

NAME PENNANT

1. Cut out a pennant from ¼ yd. of felt, approx. 9" x 22" x 22".
2. Cut out a 9" x 2" strip from the same piece and fold this over the base of the pennant. Sew it down.
3. Cut out letters of your child's name (3"-4" high).
4. Glue letters onto pennant.
5. Glue on other decorations.

ART CENTER

Include:

■ a small table and chair at which your child can work.

■ a special drawer in which to store all of the art supplies together. If no drawer is available, use a sturdy carton. You and your child can decorate it with original artwork.

■ a place to display your child's artistic efforts. Tack them on a bulletin board, for instance. You can make one out of a sheet of white insulation styrofoam board from a building supply store. Cut it to any shape (maybe your child's first initial).

■ art supplies—crayons, scissors, watercolors, brushes, paper, paste for a start.

READING NOOK

Include:

■ a shelf within easy reach filled with lots of books. Be sure to keep your child's own books separate from those taken from the library.

■ a good light—try one that clips on.

■ a comfortable chair—kids love beanbag chairs, and they're not expensive.

THINKING/DREAMING/RELAXING SPOT

Include:

■ any comfortable place on which to plop—bed pillows, chair, or a shaggy rug.

■ mobiles, plants, flowers (real or tissue).

Preschool classrooms are often organized into art, music, and reading areas, too. When a child works in these areas, it is not to train him to become a famous artist, a great musician, or a scholar. His teachers are helping that happy, healthy, independent individual I spoke about earlier to develop. Early Childhood professionals know that children develop many skills and concepts through activities that are not directly related to the activity itself. Therefore, throughout this book, there are many art, music, and reading experiences. Even if you're not "arty," "musical," or a "bookworm," don't pass them up. They're fun, easy, and of real educational value to your child.

Private places

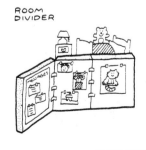

ROOM DIVIDER

If your child shares a room, consider putting a curtain or room divider down the middle of the room in order to provide privacy for each occupant. A simple, inexpensive one to make uses three sheets of white, styrofoam insulation board that are hinged together with straight pins and two by four feet pieces of fabric (six pieces—three for each side).

Sometimes, however, extra space is hard to find. But if you believe it is really important for each child to have a place to call his own, you'll think of new, creative ways to find that space. Here are some more ideas.

■ Put a large, fluffy pillow and blanket under a table covered with a long tablecloth.

■ Turn a table on one side with its legs against the wall.

■ Tape pieces of cardboard together to create a screen—this can turn a corner of a room into a very private place.

■ After removing the flaps, place a cardboard carton (appliance box)—large enough for your child to fit into comfortably—on its side in the middle of a large room. Line the bottom with something soft—pillows or an old crib or playpen mattress. Clip a lamp on the side.

■ Pitch a small tent outside.

■ Cover two chairs that are close together with a sheet.

■ Build a tree house. Check the library for books that give complete instructions.

In each of the above, make sure that the space is comfortable to sit or lie in. Include some stuffed animals and books. And, remember—most of these can be easily taken down.

Also, be sure to listen with patience to your child's own ideas about the kind of places he would like to create. Perhaps he'd like a special plant, picture, or toy for his private place.

Don't intrude. If you want your child to understand YOUR need for privacy, respect his. Read <u>Evan's Corner</u> by Elizabeth Storr and <u>I Play in My Room</u> by Anne and Harlow Rockwell together and share your feelings about privacy.

These cozy places and organized spaces are a godsend when you need time to yourself. They also fill your child's need for the security of a place to call his own—a place to be quiet or creative and a place for which he is responsible.

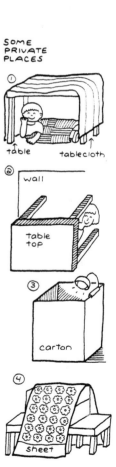

SOME PRIVATE PLACES

① table   tablecloth

② wall / table top

③ carton

④ sheet

Organizing Your Time

You are a busy adult as well as a parent. There are many things you must—or like to—do each day, but they are not always the same things, nor always in the same order. You need flexibility in your day and you want your child to be comfortable with your different activities, changes in plans, and new experiences. Young children, however, need a framework in which to deal with these unfamiliar situations; they need routines they can count on in order to feel secure and confident enough to try all the exciting adventures in store for them. A few routines will make that unusual day at the mall or a house full of strange visitors easier to adjust to. Routines can go to Grandma's overnight or on a week's vacation, too.

The roots of independence are found in security. Simple routines at the start of the day, at mealtimes, at bathtime, and at bedtime give your child a sense of grounding. They have another advantage, too. Children learn to be independent by practicing the same things over and over. In this way, they first master one skill or concept and are ready and confident to go on to the next one. Through routines, your child gets lots of practice with basic skills in familiar situations.

Routines need not be dull. The rest of this chapter gives you helpful hints and suggestions for making routines rich, learning experiences for your child.

TOGETHER

Help your child learn about sequence and routines by making a My Day Book. As you make this foldout book/clock, talk about the things all people do each day, like eating and sleeping. If your child is in a preschool program, this might be a good opportunity to talk about his routines away from home.

A word now about children, routines, and time. Young children are not bound by exact times on the clock. For example, your child does not need to take a bath at 5:30 each evening to feel secure. In fact, very few young children have any idea when 5:30 is. He just needs to take his bath after dinner and before bedtime on most days.

Rather than by clock or calendar time, your child's world is probably separated into "playtime," "bathtime," "bedtime," and so on. Slowly, he begins to understand that the same, or similar, sequences are repeated over and over, as he goes from day to night to the next day. Through this realization, he develops a sense that time is measured by days and nights.

The concept of time is very complicated for young children. The relationships of space and sequence, necessary for understanding time, develop slowly over the first nine or ten years of a person's life. Routines are especially helpful in developing the skill of time sequencing—the first step in understanding how time works.

Right now, your child's sense of duration—how long—is probably related to interest. If he doesn't like taking a nap, naptime is a long time. If he loves to take a bath, bathtime is a short time.

He won't be able to put together time sequencing, duration, space, movement, and clocktime until he is nine or ten. You can help in his preschool

MY DAY BOOK

YOU'LL NEED:

 scissors

 paper plate

paper scraps— for clock hands

brass fastener

felt tip marker

crayons

colored pencils

 ruler

WHAT TO DO:

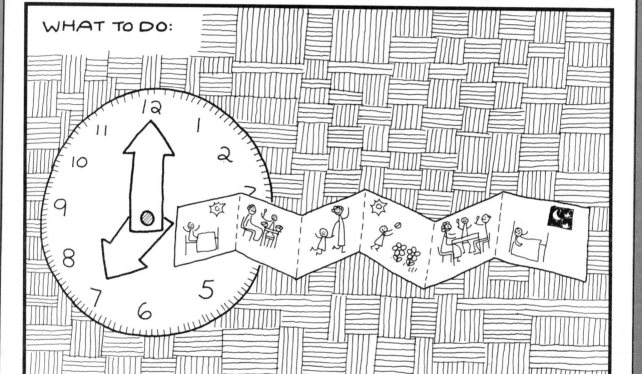

1.
Cut a piece of construction paper in half lengthwise and tape the 2 halves together to make a 4½" x 24" strip. Accordion-fold strip to make a fold-out book.

2.
Make a clock face, using a paper plate, marker, paper hands, and a brass fastener.

3.
Have your child draw pictures showing daily routines—in sequence from morning to night. Move hands of clock to correspond with time of day.

years, however, by giving him sequential routines, working on number concepts, and using precise words to help him develop a time vocabulary. Even though he won't really understand what the words mean yet, he will begin to associate the words with time. *"Five more minutes and it will be time for lunch. I'll set the timer on the stove so you'll know when it's time to eat."*

Use time words like "minute," "hour," "day," "night," "week," "month," "year," "watch, " "clock," "calendar," "winter," "spring," "summer," and "fall" so that your child can become familiar with them through his daily activities.

Try to be exact when you talk about time. That's not as easy as it sounds. Just think for a moment about some of the phrases we use to describe the passage of time: *"Just a moment. . ." "I'll be right back." "It's been a long time. . ." "See you later."*

The phrases above mean something different each time they are used. When your child asks you a question and you're on the phone, do you ever say *"Be with you in a minute"*? Is that *"minute"* often five or even fifteen minutes? One alternative is to say instead *"I know you have something to ask me; I'll be with you as soon as I finish on the phone."* The pressure is off you because you've acknowledged your child's need; at the same time, you haven't confused his notion of time.

Another phrase often used by busy parents is *"We'll do it soon"* in answer to their child's request to go to the zoo or do a special project. A calendar is a good tool for changing *"soon"* from a disappointingly vague promise into something to which your child can look forward.

To reinforce the passage of time on a calendar until the day of a special event, you can put beans or buttons in a jar, one for each day until the special one arrives. Your child can take out a bean each day and actually "see" the time passing—the big day coming closer. An hourglass also helps young children understand the passage of time visually.

When a special event is coming up in the near future, you can make a SURPRISE CALENDAR for your child. *You'll need:* poster board or fabric, and theme stickers or picture cutouts from greeting cards. First, make a little door for each day between now and the special event. Then, behind each door, on a backing, put a different sticker or picture. Either number the doors in sequence or put the calendar date on each. Each day, have your child open the appropriate door. You might want to coordinate the pictures with a little treat or game. For example, when your child opens the door with the picture of a lion behind it, he might have to find his toy lion that you have hidden.

SURPRISE CALENDAR

A calendar also helps your child with the other concepts related to time. Suddenly, "day," "week," and "month" are right there in front of him, and he gets a real sense of them as he marks them off. He can "see" and even "feel"—when he marks it off—that a week is longer than two days and a month is longer than a week.

There are some charming books you can read together that will also reinforce these time concepts. All Day Long by Richard Scarry focuses on daily routines; Pamela Jane's Week by Alberta Robison talks about what goes on during seven days in the life of a little girl; Chicken Soup with Rice by Maurice Sendak and Anno's Counting Book by Mitsumasa Anno bring new color and fun to the months of the year. Around the Year by Tasha Tudor is another good book for discussing the months and seasons.

Calendars are particularly useful for children with divorced parents who often have special problems with time because of being shuttled back and forth between two homes. Their situation often causes them to feel a frustrating lack of control over their lives. A calendar gives them back a little control and security by presenting them with a clear, visual understanding of when they will be with Mom and when they will have time with Dad.

There are lots of charming calendars that can be bought and displayed in a prominent place in your child's room. Each night before going to bed, have him mark off the day that has just passed. Since young children tend to live completely in the present, calendars give them a better sense of past and future. If possible, have your child make a picture on the calendar that shows what he did that day. This aids his recall skills and his understanding of the passage of time. Sharing experiences is especially beneficial if you haven't spent the whole day together. (This might be an excellent routine for working parents to set up.)

Calendars also can be made by you and your child and used to develop skills and concepts other than time.

▶ Make your own calendar together to use month by month. On the first day of each month, get together to draw a picture; make an appropriate montage of pictures of the season cut from old magazines; or create a display of pressed leaves or flowers. Then, plan some special times together during the month and mark the dates on a handmade or commercial calendar month. Paste it to your artwork.

▶ Your child can keep a weather chart. Each day he can draw symbols or use weather stamps, available in stores, for a sunny, rainy, or cloudy day.

Whether you buy or make your calendar, be sure that the numbers are large enough for your child to practice reading them and that there is enough room in the daily spaces for him to draw or place a sticker.

WEATHER STAMPS

1. Cut a SUN, CLOUD SNOW-FLAKE, and RAIN CLOUD from inner tube tire or sheet of packing foam.

2. Glue each shape onto a wood scrap.

3. Use with a stamp pad or printing ink.

Morning Routines

It's 7:00 am—or 7:30, or 8:00—the start of an exciting new day for you and your child. Most days are exciting for young children; there's always something new to see, to experience, to learn. You're really starting off ahead of the game—nine times out of ten, your child is expecting to have a good day; he is looking forward to whatever you have in store for him.

If possible, have a wake–up routine. If your child is an early riser (earlier than you), be clear about what you expect him to do until you wake up. Some children love to use this time, when all is quiet, to look at their books for a little while. You can encourage this, especially on weekends. On the other hand, if your child has a real problem getting out of bed in the morning, try waking him ten minutes early; then, climb into his bed, cuddle, and read a story together to help him make the transition from sleep to activity. Try Sunshine by Jan Ormerod, Milton, the Early Riser by Robert Kraus, Good Morning, Baby Bear by Eric Hill, or My Good Morning Book by Eloise Wilkin to make sure your child gets up "on the right side of the bed."

Have an early morning routine. Your child will appreciate knowing what's in store. Whether it's breakfast, brushing teeth, getting dressed and out the door, or brushing teeth, getting dressed, breakfast, and, then, playtime, be consistent.

Choosing which clothes to wear.

Choosing which parts go together

Getting dressed

Getting dressed is an important time for a young child. A lot of learning can go on during this seemingly simple routine. Children can begin dressing themselves at a very early age. You can encourage this process by showing them what to do over and over, if necessary, and by being enthusiastic about the whole process. *"Some day soon, you will be able to do this all by yourself."* As early as two years of age, children can decide between one shirt and another and can put on uncomplicated pieces of clothing by themselves. Almost all three–year–olds can put on shoes by themselves (with help in matching shoes and feet and tying). About this time, they can really begin to dress themselves completely.

The style of clothing a child wears will have a big influence on how quickly he will be able to dress himself. For young children, pants and skirts that pull on, rather than buttoning or zipping, make getting dressed much easier. You may want to put Velcro on some articles of clothing instead of buttons or snaps. However, children will have to learn to work the buttons, snaps, and zippers eventually, so, some should include both options.

When buying clothes, pay close attention to how they fit and are fastened. Shorts or shoes that are slightly too tight or pants with hard-to-operate buttons or heavy snaps above the fly can be frustrating to little hands just mastering their fine motor control.

Choosing the clothes to be worn is an important part of getting dressed. When a child is beginning to do this all on his own, try not to be critical when he matches stripes and plaids.

There are a few "tricks of the trade" that help children dress themselves more easily. The most popular of these is the Montessori method for putting on coats and jackets. In this method, your child puts his coat on the floor with the collar closest to his feet. By putting his hands in the sleeves and flipping the coat over his head, he can put on his coat with no help at a very young age.

Choosing what clothes fit the weather

The key word in the whole process is, as in so many things, PATIENCE. If possible, allow a little extra time so that no one will be under pressure. There will be days, however, when your child will be tired or not feeling well, and will ask for help. In these cases, of course, lend a helping hand.

Since being able to dress himself is such an important part of your child's overall self-image, you really need to encourage this step toward independence. The feelings that keep a child from taking this step eagerly are easy to understand, however. The rituals and routine of getting dressed are part of a time when adults and children are very close because no matter how busy you may be at other times, you are always available then. Your child, quite understandably, may be disappointed when he can no longer count on that special time together. Try to keep it a "together routine" for as long as possible, even though your role will change to that of an observer.

There are lots of things you two can discuss while your child is getting dressed. There are many skills your child can be developing besides the motor skills used in pulling on, buttoning, and zipping up.

With patience, enthusiasm, and a little time invested, it won't be too long before your child tells you with confidence and pride, *"Don't help me. I can do it."*

Fastening buttons and tying shoes.

Being aware of patterns in design of clothing

Choosing matching colors.

Going to school

If your child is going to a preschool program or a day-care center, early morning is an especially important time. It sets the tone for the whole day. Try to plan your time to avoid mad dashes to the car or school bus and to allow for some calm, cheerful talk—perhaps on your lap—and lots of hugs and cuddles.

If going to school or day-care is a fact of life, allow your child to make some decisions each morning in areas where he does have a choice. He'll feel more in control of his life if he can choose between eggs or cereal for breakfast or a green or red pencil in his knapsack. Keep the choices simple—between two or three things. Make sure that you can accept whatever he chooses.

Especially in the beginning, encourage your child to bring something to school from home—a stuffed animal or favorite book or toy (clearly labeled with his name). This reminder of home will make him feel much more comfortable and secure.

When you take your child to school or the bus stop, you may hear "*I want you to stay here today*" or "*I'm not going.*" Be a good listener and let your child know that it's okay to feel uneasy about making the transition from home to school. Try not to make statements like "*School is so much fun. You'll feel better later.*" "Later" means nothing to that unhappy preschooler, who feels bad NOW. Sometimes, fears about the big school bus can be part of the problem. Read Big Paul's School Bus by Paul Nichols to your child. It's written by a bus driver and addresses many concerns a young child might have.

If you are taking your child to school, make it clear what the two of you will be doing when you arrive. When you arrive, the routines of going into the school hand-in-hand and hanging up his coat together can be very reassuring.

Always let your child know when you are leaving. Tell him what you will be doing while he is at school. Ask him what he thinks he will be doing with his teacher and the other children. Make the time discussion as concrete as possible. If you know your child's schedule, you can say something like "*First, you will play in the block corner; next, you will hear a story; then, you will have a snack; at the end, I'll be back to pick you up.*" If your child is in a day-care setting, be sure to let the caregiver know when you will return. Many children get upset near the end of the day, and the caregiver can reassure them if she knows your plans. Try very hard not to be late.

A good beginning sets the tone for a good day for all of us. On school days, that good beginning starts at home and follows your child right into his classroom.

Time to Take a Bath

A bath in a shallow, warm tub in a well-heated room with an adult on hand can provide a safe, no mess, exploration time for your child. While it will help your child to look forward to this routine at a regular time in the sequence of the day, you should feel free to use bathtime whenever you need it—to relax your child, to change his mood, or just to clean him off when he comes in from splashing in puddles.

For babies, the bath can repeat the secure feelings of the prebirth experience in the womb. For toddlers, the joy of making ripples, poking fingers, dipping and soaking, is never-ending. With your toddler, you can read <u>Sam's Bath</u> by Barbro Lindgren.

For the three–year–old, actively exploring his world, the bathtub becomes a place to experiment with pouring, ladling, and funneling. Given a little time and space, he can imitate Mom and Dad washing the dishes, the car, or the laundry. He can pretend to be a sailor or a fisherman and go anywhere his imagination takes him. He will enjoy <u>The Bathtub Ocean</u> by Diane Paterson.

Bath toys should include a washcloth, rubber toys, a doll to bathe, and various kitchen utensils. Measuring spoons, a baster, funnel, empty squeeze bottles of various sizes, ladle—all provide lots of opportunities for experimentation. Introduce just a few of these at a time. (Water play can continue in the kitchen sink, on a smaller scale, or outside in a plastic pool.)

One of the most popular areas in the preschool classroom is the water table. Children learn math and science concepts there as well as developing language and social skills. You can get your child off to a good start on these concepts and skills in the bathtub. Best of all, water play is nonthreatening because it doesn't require any special skills. It makes no demands on your child, leaving him free to use it to meet his needs.

Four- and five-year-old scientists make exciting discoveries in the bathtub through free exploration and a little guidance. Finding out which container holds more water, as he pours some from one to the other or seeing what floats and what sinks are all perfect experiments for your preschooler.

HELPFUL HINTS: You can help keep water in the tub by keeping the bath water level low. Try to keep the soaping and shampooing until the end, so that bubble blowing and underwater exploration can be safe activities earlier.

The bathtub scientist

Children like to experiment in water and can do so with a few household odds and ends. This allows them to discover firsthand what water does to things and how objects behave in water.

Here are some experiments you can explore together while your child is playing in the bathtub.

■ *What happens to paper in the bath water? To cellophane? To tinfoil?*
■ *If you crunch up the tinfoil into a small ball, will it float?*
■ *Do soap bubbles last longer on cellophane or tinfoil?*
■ *What happens to an ice cube in the bath? Does it float?*

Talk about what sinks and floats in the tub. Divide up the tub toys and kitchen utensils into those that float and those that do not. Ask your child why he thinks this happens. Try to have him compare the size, weight, and/or material of the objects.

Try some experiments, using plastic locking bags.

▶ Fill a bag halfway with water. Ask: *"What color is the water?"*
▶ Fill a bag halfway with water and lock it. Have your child tip it every which way. (He will discover that the water keeps level—horizontal to the ground.)
▶ Fill the bag with water and close the top. Put two pinholes in the bag—one at the top and one near the bottom. Have your child squeeze and let the water squirt out. *"Through which hole does the water squirt out farther?"*
▶ Have your child look at his hand through the water in the bag. Talk about how things look when you see them through the water. If possible, challenge your child to look under water in the bath without the bag (getting his face wet) at his own feet or hands. (This is an important step in learning to swim.)

It is important to talk with your child about how water can be contained. Have him experiment with scooping water with his hand, then both hands; finally, using a cup or jar. Have him fill a container with water, using a measuring spoon and then a cup. Through this type of water play, your child is developing such skills as pouring and measuring.

For a musical bath, try washing with a song. To the tune of *"If You're Happy and You Know It. . .,"* sing *"If You're Dirty and You Know It. Wash your (hands, face, neck, legs, arms. . .)."* This is a tuneful way to learn body parts and, also, to wash some less popular areas, like ears, without a fuss.

The bathtub swimmer

Your child's first swimming lessons usually involve just getting wet and enjoying the water. Fun experiences in the bathtub make this a lot easier. Let your child splash around in a shallow bath; have him be an elephant taking a bath by scooping up water with his trunk (hands) and dumping it on his head. If he will let you, pour some water on his head, and show him how to wipe it out of his eyes. Ninety percent of most toddler swimming class-time is spent encouraging children to get their faces wet.

TOGETHER

Make Sink and Float Boats and experiment with pebble cargoes. Follow up with Sink and Float Dessert on page 73.

SINK AND FLOAT BOATS

YOU'LL NEED:

 styrofoam egg carton

 styrofoam meat tray

 ½ walnut shell

 sponge-like foam pieces

 aluminum pie pan

 milk carton container (cut in half)

 thin dowels and blunt toothpicks

pebbles

 tape

plasticine clay

 paper

scissors

WHAT TO DO:

 1. Set out materials listed above.

 2. With a little adult help, your child can assemble boats. Paper sails can be added to thin dowels or blunt toothpicks and stuck in place with plasticene.

 3. Test the boats in water. See and discuss how much pebble "cargo" each boat can carry.

The next lesson your child should learn is to blow bubbles. If this skill is taught early in the tub and practiced often, he will have an easy time in a pool with the rhythmic breathing of the crawl, when he is ready for it. You can try some of the basic games used to teach blowing bubbles in clean bath water.

▶ Have your child blow bubbles in the water, using a very short or cut-off straw. Using the abbreviated straw encourages blowing bubbles and splashes water in his face as well.

▶ Have your child pretend to blow out birthday candles (your fingers) above the water level. When he is comfortable with the idea, lower your hand and then your fingers into the water so he is blowing out the candles with his face in the water. He'll make some terrific bubbles.

▶ Have him blow bubbles and make the noise of a motorboat at the same time as a toy boat floats around the tub.

If the tub is large enough, suggest to your child that he lie on his tummy and kick his feet like a swimmer. Help him straighten his legs as he kicks. You might want to count the number of kicks together.

These are all suggested games for your child, NOT lessons. Keep them fun and relaxed and you will be amazed at his ability when it comes time for formal lessons.

TOGETHER

For an artistic experience, make Soap Crayons to use in the bathtub. Your child can draw pictures, letters, and numbers, which wash off easily and leave a clean slate for the next time.

SOAP CRAYONS

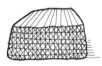

YOU'LL NEED:

food coloring | water | mild powder laundry soap | teaspoon | measuring cup | plastic ice cube tray

WHAT TO DO:

1. Fill a measuring cup to "1 cup" mark with laundry soap.

2. Add 30-40 drops of food coloring.

3. Add water by teaspoonful until soap is liquid. Stir well.

4. Pack soap into ice cube tray.

5. Set in a sunny, dry, place for 2 days.

6. Crayons will become hard and great for writing in the sink or tub.

...o Have a Meal

Mealtimes should be happy routines for your child. Pleasant eating experiences are as important as nutritious foods. Food habits and attitudes toward eating are largely formed during the preschool years. Yet, mealtimes are real battlegrounds between many parents and their young children. Have you ever heard *"This is yucky!"* *"I won't eat this; my meat is touching the rice,"* or *"Granny lets me eat candy for breakfast at her house."* After working hard to prepare a good, nutritious meal, statements like these can make you want to shout, bribe, lecture, or threaten—which usually makes things worse.

How do you make mealtimes happy times for everyone at the table? Here are some suggestions from parenting expert Sherry Burrell.

Before the meal

▶ At playtime, let your child pretend to cook a dinner for you. Children who enjoy this activity will also enjoy pretending when you are doing the "real cooking." (More on this in Chapter 4.)

▶ Together read <u>Bread and Jam for Frances</u> by Russell Hoban. It's an excellent book about a little girl who refuses to eat anything except bread and jam. It has a happy, instructive ending, of course.

▶ Provide quiet activities just before meals—books, records, puzzles, play dough, and so on. It can be very difficult for your child suddenly to sit still at the table after being very active.

▶ Whenever possible, involve your child in preparing or serving meals. Remember that children are enthusiastic helpers.

▶ Try to serve the food right away after your child is seated. A waiting child will entertain himself with whatever is in reach if he has to wait too long.

During the meal

▶ If possible, serve foods "family style" so that your child can learn to decide how much to put on his plate. If you do dish up your child's portions, it is better to give small servings and allow for seconds than to overwhelm him with large portions at the beginning.

▶ Permit your child to make choices about what he will eat. When introducing new foods, offer him taste-sized portions. Avoiding pressure to try the new food will allow your child to decide to try it.

▶ Stay away from the "clean plate club" idea. Instead, focus on helping children learn to take servings they will finish.

▶ At the table, create an atmosphere of acceptance and respect for your child. Include him in the family conversation and make sure he has a chance to be the center of attention in an enjoyable way some of the time.

▶ If your child leaves the table to play or throws food, he has signaled that he is through with his meal. Have a quiet discussion with him—not at mealtime—to make this rule simple and clear. Be sure your child understands it. Then, when it happens again, remove your child's plate and calmly let him know that he has shown that he is through with eating.

TOGETHER

Copy the place mat and setting at the right (or design your own) to have your child make his very own special mat.

A PLACE MAT

YOU'LL NEED:

 11"x14" piece of paper

 clear contact paper

 scissors

 crayons and markers

 old magazines

 GLUE

My Name

WHAT TO DO:

 1. Draw an empty place mat setting on an 11" x 14" piece of paper.

 2. Have your child draw or cut out and paste on magazine pictures of his favorite foods on the empty plates, in the bowl, and glass.

 3. Cover the whole page with clear contact paper and use as a real place mat.

▶ Most important, remember to look for behavior you can encourage during the meal. All too often, we forget to "pat our children on the back" when their behavior isn't causing a problem.

Mealtime fun and learning

▶ **SETTING THE TABLE** This can be a wonderful learning experience for your child. It involves following directions *"Put a fork at every place"*; counting *"You need to get four forks"*; and one-to-one correspondence *"Each one gets a fork, a knife, and a spoon."*

Instead of asking your child to perform all of these steps himself the first time, start by setting the table yourself and having him perform one of the steps. If he is successful, he can add one more the next time. Don't rush it. Remember that success is the key to joyful learning. After he has mastered two or three steps, have him practice these for a week, just to feel comfortable—and successful.

▶ **THINGS TO TALK ABOUT** Serving meals is a great lesson in sequence. Even if your child does not serve each course, talk about what comes first, next, and last in the meal.

Have your child describe some activities in his day to the whole family during the meal. This will give him practice in recall and sequence with a little help from you. Have other family members talk about their day. If the events have been significant and the sequence pretty obvious, ask your child to remember the highlights and even the sequence *"What did Daddy do after lunch?"* Any way you can help sharpen your child's listening skills will be very useful for later learning. Make these conversations low key and not a quiz. They should be fun and interesting—not pressured or threatening.

The dinner table is a great place to talk about important concepts and develop language skills—colors, textures, tastes, and smells of the foods—all of these give your child practice in using his senses and finding the right words to describe sensations.

Your child might like to interview family members to find out their favorite foods. Then, you can make copies of the empty place setting for him to use in creating a place mat for each person. If you cover them with contact paper, you'll have a set of family place mats. These make great personal gifts for relatives, friends, and teachers.

Time to Go to Bed

Bedtime is an important time for developing good parent-child relationships. It is a time for sharing, especially if you work or your child has been out of the home in a day-care center or preschool program. But, along with talk and sharing, fears often come out at this quiet time before sleep.

The idea of going to sleep can awaken many fears in young children. Nightmares usually begin around age three and reach their height when a child is between the ages of four and a half and five years old. Your child doesn't find excuses not to go to bed merely because he wants to be sociable—or a nuisance; experts believe that sleep is often frightening to a young child because it means separation from the adults upon whom he depends. Your child probably resists going to bed because he doesn't want to be alone. When he finally falls asleep, he often has nightmares which are his way of coping with his fears about being small and helpless. These fears are played out and mastered at night through dreams in much the same way he deals with them during the day by acting out different roles and situations.

Encourage your child to talk about his fears and dreams if he remembers them. Putting feelings into words makes them less frightening and more manageable. Don't try to explain anything in rational, grown-up terms. Just listen calmly and sympathetically and make sure your child knows that you understand how frightening his dreams are for him and that, no matter what, you will keep him safe.

Routines at bedtime give your child added security to face the darkness and any giants or monsters who may be hiding under his bed. Find an activity that calms your child— whether it is singing, a back rub, or a story read aloud. There are some lovely books written about bedtime and dreaming that you can share.

- A Child's Good Night Book by Margaret Wise Brown
- Good Night Moon by Margaret Wise Brown
- Wake Up and Good Night by Charlotte Zolotow
- The Sleepy Book by Charlotte Zolotow
- Moonlight by Jan Ormerod
- Close Your Eyes by Jean Marzollo

If you provide certain routines during each day, for getting dressed, bathtime, mealtimes, and bedtime, your child will be a lot more flexible about the rest of the day. He will be much more willing to fit himself into your schedule if he knows that certain events occur pretty much at the same time in the sequence of the day. If the events themselves have a reassuring sameness to them, like almost always eating dinner family style, always taking a bath in the evening with the same rubber duck, always singing the same quiet song with Dad right before lights out, your child will feel confident to explore new experiences and develop independence.

EVERYDAY CHORES 3

Household skills

Language skills while

you clean

Math around the house

The science of cleaning

Learning in the laundry

Household Skills

You have many jobs to do during your day. If you are like me, you have cleaning, tidying up, taking care of pets, watering house plants, doing the laundry, and so on. You have all of these to consider, and that's before you step into the kitchen—the next chapter—or out the front door. That's also before you consider the energetic, enthusiastic little person who wants to be a part of everything you do.

You want your child to be happy and healthy, but, you NEED him to be independent if you're ever to get everything done. Luckily, you can help your child become independent and get your daily chores done at the same time. Look again at the ways to help your child move toward independence on page 18. One of the most important pieces of advice I can give you is to let your child help whenever possible.

So, sit down and make a list of the things your child can do to help in each area. That list might include such jobs as: putting away his toys, changing the pillowcases when you are changing sheets, dusting tables, watering house plants with a small watering can, or feeding the pets.

There are many things your child can do, and wanting to help is a real sign of growing up. It's usually easier to "do it yourself," but you shouldn't dampen that bubbly enthusiasm. And, after all, your child needs some kind of activity to do while you work.

You can create a helper kit by assembling household items that your child can use to work alongside you or alone in dramatic play. For a CLEANER KIT, *you'll need:* pump bottles filled with water, squeegee, sponge, dusting cloth or feather duster, dusting mop (the handle can be cut down), smock or apron, and scrub brush. Place all of these into a plastic container with a handle or a six-pack soda carton.

APRON and SMOCKS

1. EASY-TO-SEW APRON

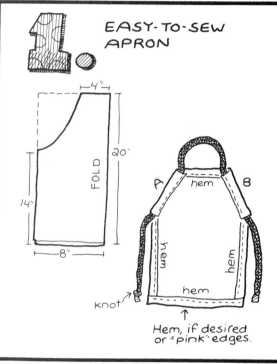

FOLD

4"
20"
14"
8"

A   hem   B

hem   hem

hem

hem

Knot

Hem, if desired or "pink" edges.

YOU'LL NEED:

- ½ yard stiff cloth - canvas or sailcloth
- 2 yards cording
- newspaper - ruler - scissors
- needle and thread or sewing machine
- OPTIONAL: pinking shears

WHAT TO DO:

1. Fold a sheet of newspaper and measure, using diagram directions.

2. Use newspaper pattern to cut out fabric apron.

3. Fold over sides A and B (see sketch) 1½": sew ¼" in from cut edge.

4. Thread cording through 1 side, up around neck and back through opposite side.

5. Knot ends.

VARIATION:

This apron can be made from clear plastic. Then, it can be sponged clean.

2. PLASTIC CARRY-ALL BAG SMOCK

3. OLD SHIRT SMOCK

Slip over head and rest straps on shoulders

Open the bottom.

Cut away sleeves.

Language skills while you clean

There are lots of things your child can be learning while you are straightening up the house. These activities offer him a change from his "same old toys." While playing with household objects, your child will be becoming more familiar with his first world—his home.

▶ For the toddler, there is a wealth of vocabulary words waiting to be learned in the bedroom, bathroom, and living room. For the older child, identify items with written labels so that he can see what words "look like." This is an important step and will help your child develop reading skills.

▶ If your child is a toddler, provide scarves, ribbon, mirror, wind-up clock, brush and comb, and other objects to explore while you work in the bedroom. In the bathroom, he can play with a clean toothbrush, a Band—Aid box, a tightly capped toothpaste tube, or empty plastic bottles. He will enjoy the shapes, textures, and the "grown-upness" of the objects. Sometimes, let your child examine them alone; other times, discuss them together. Demonstrate their use. Use towels and scarves to hide objects and have your child guess what's hidden. Above all, name items over and over.

▶ Be sure to point out the household objects in books and magazines. Then, while you're working, give your child a magazine, name a familiar object, and have him hunt for it on a particular page or, for an older child, through several pages.

▶ With a preschooler, there are many games you can play with words and household objects. Ask your child to get things for you, first in the room you both are in, and then later, when you are in a different room. He has to remember where to find them. (Identifying groups of objects in certain rooms is a beginning step of classifying.)

▶ Put a few items in out-of-the-usual places and let your child tell you what is wrong and where they really belong. *"The toothbrush belongs in the bathroom, not on the pillow in the bedroom."* (This is another game which helps your child practice classifying.)

▶ While you work, play "I'm Thinking of. . ." with your child. Describe something for him to guess with as few clues as possible. Describe its color, shape, texture, how the item is used, and in what room it can be found.

▶ "Touch by Ten" is a variation on "I'm Thinking of. . ." Your child learns about attributes of objects and practices making his own descriptions. Begin by choosing an object in the room and saying *"I'm going to count to ten. When I start to count, I want you to find something in this room that is shiny (or smooth or green or furry). When you find something shiny, leave your hand on it. 1, 2, 3. . .10. Did you find something shiny? Tell me all about it."* Through this game, your child develops his descriptive vocabulary, learns to follow directions, and soon, can become the leader in "I'm Thinking of. . .," giving you the clues.

▶ "Sarah Says" is a variation on "Simon Says," which uses only positive commands and allows you to give them verbally, without demonstration. Your

Puppets are wonderful tools to help your child develop language, express feelings, and expand his imagination. With a puppet in hand, he will find it easy to make up a name, personality, and stories about this special character. Quickie Puppets are so quick and easy to make that, in no time at all, your child will have a "new playmate,"— who can do the "talking"—and free you to do household chores. Puppets also develop your child's hand-eye coordination.

QUICKIE PUPPETS

YOU'LL NEED:

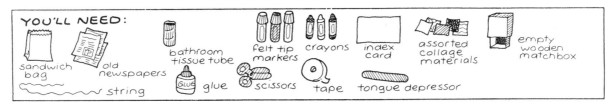

sandwich bag, old newspapers, bathroom tissue tube, felt tip markers, crayons, index card, assorted collage materials, empty wooden matchbox, glue, scissors, tape, tongue depressor, string

WHAT TO DO:

PAPER BAG AND PAPER TUBE PUPPET

string
bathroom tissue tube

1. Stuff a sandwich bag full with newspaper.
2. Decorate bag with markers, crayons, and/or glued-on collage materials.
3. Attach to bathroom tissue tube with string.

INDEX CARD PUPPET

1. Squeeze an index card so it curves in the middle for a mouth.
2. Use a marker to draw the tongue.
3. Glue on or draw on features.

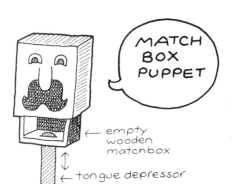

MATCH BOX PUPPET

empty wooden matchbox
tongue depressor

1. Decorate an empty wooden matchbox with felt tip markers.
2. Make a slot in drawer part of matchbox.
3. Tape tongue depressor to slot in drawer. Use it to open and close the mouth.

child will learn body parts and how to follow directions, as you say *"Sarah says: pat your head. . . touch your toes. . . hop in a circle"*—and you can be cleaning the ring on the bathtub! Play this game until your child loses interest or use it to make an easy transition to the next activity: *"Sarah says wash your hands and sit down for lunch."*

▶ Sometimes, your mood and/or your child's dictates a less serious game. Have fun with words; be silly. Bring objects alive by guessing what they might say if they could talk. *"What might the flowers have to say when you water them?" "What might the mop say to the wet floor?"* This helps your child stretch his imagination and develop his creativity.

Language learning begins at home. The activities above keep your child occupied while you work around the house. At the same time he is building vocabulary and language skills.

Math around the house

Your home is full of items your child can use to practice math skills. Counting, classifying, recognizing numbers, understanding numerical relationships, and measuring are among the skills that your child can explore and practice while you are working around the house.

Probably without realizing it, you have been introducing your child to math concepts around the house for a long time. *"Put your hands on your two ears"* you say in a game; and your child is developing a general sense of the number two through touch. When you tell him to take two cookies, he is further exploring the concept of twoness. When you pose the problem *"I have one piece of pink paper and two children who want to use it,"* you are not only providing an experience in sharing, you are introducing your child to the process of division.

▶ Children love to measure things. At a young age, they notice things only in relation to themselves. You are used to measuring things in units, such as inches, feet, and miles. Your child, on the other hand, measures according to comparisons at first—identifying things that are the same as his foot, his pinkie, or his height. Next, he begins to understand the concepts of *longer* and *shorter.* Finally, he can distinguish between concepts, such as *big, bigger,* and *biggest.*

You have many objects that will help give your child practice in math:
■ clock—number recognition, measurement of time
■ money—counting, exchange values—five pennies equal a nickel
■ telephone—number recognition, numbers in sequence
■ ruler or yardstick—number recognition, measurement of height, width, and length
■ thermometer—number recognition, measurement of temperature
■ radio or TV—number recognition

TOGETHER

Since personal measurements are so natural with young children, make Personal Measuring Tools with your child. Have him use them to compare sizes, measure things around the house, and notice growth— in plants, his own body, and even the family pet, if you can keep it still long enough.

PERSONAL MEASURING TOOLS

YOU'LL NEED:

 colored lightweight cardboard (or posterboard)

 pencil - for tracing

 scissors

 string or non-stretchy ribbon

 hole puncher

 stapler

 metal ring - 1 for each set of tools

WHAT TO DO:

1. Trace your child's hand and foot on cardboard. Cut out and punch a hole right at wrist and heel.
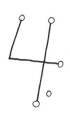

2. Use string to get your child's height. Cut it off. Staple to a piece of cardboard.
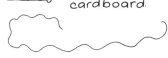

3. Attach measuring tools to a metal ring.

4. Use hand and foot measurements to see how tall a plant has grown. Record and remeasure a week apart.

5. Use string measurement to see how a tree trunk has grown. Record and remeasure a month apart. Is there any noticeable change?

6. Place a small animal, such as a gerbil or worm, on the hand or foot tool to compare size.

Let your child explore these items, and, then, set up some simple guided experiences.

▶ Help your child find all of the numbers in a room—on the clock, telephone, phone book, envelope, typewriter, or pages in a book.
▶ Have him sort many objects, according to one attribute at a time—buttons, books, blocks, boxes, bottles (nonbreakable); and those are just the Bs.

The science of cleaning

You use soap and water to clean your house. You can also use soap and water to create wonderfully fun learning experiences for your child—with bubbles!

You probably have on hand the materials necessary to make BUBBLES. *You'll need:* liquid soap, warm water, a small plastic container to hold the soapy water solution, a tray or tabletop, and different objects for blowing bubbles.

To introduce your child to the art of bubbleblowing, give him a cup or small container, half-filled with a soap-and-water solution, and a plastic straw. Encourage him to blow into the solution with the straw. A heap of bubbles will soon appear. If you cut the end of the straw in the shape of a cross, your child will blow big bubbles.

For another bubble-filled activity, wet a tray or tabletop with water. Have your child dip a cardboard tube or juice can, opened at both ends, in the soapy solution and then blow bubbles directly onto the wet surface. The bubbles will stick to the surface and even to his hand, if it is wet.

Try other objects through which to blow bubbles. Dip the wide end of a funnel into soapy water and have your child blow through the narrow end. He will make giant bubbles.

You can make gigantic bubbles—outdoors or in the basement—with this recipe. Mix ten ounces commercial bubble-making solution and two ounces glycerine (available at drugstores) together. Stir gently and avoid froth. Pour into a jelly roll pan. If the solution becomes foamy, blow gently on the surface to get rid of the froth. Put a few squirts of dishwashing liquid—one with good grease-cutting action—in the solution to break up the fat-derived glycerine. Unwind the neck of a wire coat hanger and bend the hanger to form an eight-inch hoop. Have your child dip the hoop into the solution completely and pull gently through the air. He can make bubbles that stretch out to four or five feet!

Challenge your child with questions like these:
■ *"What size bubble did you make?"*

DON'T THROW IT AWAY!

DON'T THROW IT AWAY... IT WILL FEED THE IMAGINATION!

Save some or all of these items. Your child will find uses for them. Add some glue, tape, markers, crayons, or paint and he will have new playthings. keep a large box filled with these items.

THINGS TO SAVE:

paper rolls oatmeal boxes	→ rocket ship
milk cartons	→ pull train
shoe boxes	→ doll house rooms
sheets	→ tent / ghosts / sleeping bag
ice cream containers	→ robots
wood scraps	→ sculpture / animals monsters
paper clips	→ necklace / jewelry
paper rolls	→ wax paper and elastic band-KAZOO / telescope / megaphone
cork, sponge, styrofoam trays, walnut shell halves	→ boats
empty frozen juice cans, string	→ telephone / stilts
egg carton, milk carton	→ castle
empty food containers	→ store
boxes	→ cage / doll bed / house
paper plates cups, napkins, plastic utensils	→ restaurant
socks, nylon stockings	→ sock puppets / old faces
paper milk containers	→ cut / blocks

THINGS TO MAKE:

■ *"Can you put two together?"*
■ *"Do you think there is anything inside the bubble?"*
■ *"What color is the bubble?"*

Bubblemaking contains many of the basic elements of science—experimenting, problem-solving, and inventing. It's a "clean" way to have fun and learn!

Learning in the laundry

Have you ever thought of laundry as a learning experience? It is for your child. There are tasks such as the following:

■ measuring detergent and water softener into a cup
■ pouring things into the machine
■ talking about how stains come out
■ observing opposites firsthand such as: *wet/dry, dirty/clean, empty/full*
■ sorting whites from colors
■ measuring how long a cycle takes on a timer
■ folding clothes
■ sorting socks
■ classifying clothes by who wears them

And, then, there is all that time when things are in the washer or dryer. You can create a CLOTHESLINE ALPHABET in your laundry area to amuse your child and to help with letter identification and small motor skills—providing good practice for cutting with scissors—while your clothes are washing or drying. *You'll need:* 26 three-by-five-inch index cards, a marker, 26 clothespins, and a clothesline.

First, hang the clothesline across the room at your child's height. Then, make a set of alphabet cards, one index card for each letter.

Let your child see how many letters he can clip on with clothespins. He must name each letter before he hangs it up. Use a small woven basket to store the letters.

If your child knows all the letters, he can start trying to place them in alphabetical order or you can challenge him to name a word that begins with each letter.

If you have old-fashioned, wooden clothespins, your child can use pipe cleaners, markers, yarn, and fabric scraps to create dolls.

Don't forget to read A Pocket for Corduroy by Don Freeman in between cycles. Talk about laundromats and the many ways to wash clothes.

MASKS

NYLON STOCKING AND HANGER MASK

YOU'LL NEED:

- 1 wire hanger
- old, clean nylon stocking
- elastic band
- assorted collage materials
- scissors
- glue

WHAT TO DO:

1. Bend wire hanger into a circle and bend hook handle closed.
2. Cover with a stocking stretched over the hanger. Secure with an elastic band.
3. Glue on hair and features.
4. Create characters and names.

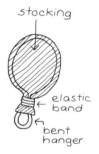

stocking

elastic band

bent hanger

BLEACH BOTTLE MASK

YOU'LL NEED:

- 1 large empty bleach bottle- rinsed and cleaned thoroughly
- scissors
- felt tip markers
- stapler or tape
- tongue depressor

WHAT TO DO:

1. Cut a mask from bleach bottle. (Use scissors for a smooth cut.)
2. Cut out eye slots.
3. Decorate with markers.
4. Staple or tape a tongue depressor to bottom.

cut

IN THE KITCHEN   4

The cooking process

The skill-ful cook

Cooking and science

A cook's tools

Math in the kitchen

The chef is an artist

Parents' snacking guide

Cookbooks for kids

The Cooking Process

If your life is anything like mine, you spend a great deal of time in the kitchen. Your child spends a lot of time in the kitchen, too, and that is good, because cooking and kitchen-related experiences are filled with learning possibilities. Math, science, language development, motor coordination, even art and music—the kitchen has it all.

You don't have to spend a lot of time setting up elaborate projects; the activities are there. Your child is probably doing them already; all he needs is little guidance from you for exciting learning to take place.

A major chunk of the time you spend in the kitchen is that period between afternoon activities and dinner. This is a particularly difficult time of the day for a young child. It is a transition time—the time before or after a major activity in the day. It is a time when your child really needs structure and direction. Think about it. Your child is tired, hungry, and quite possibly cranky, after an active time at school or playing in the park. Maybe he has just come home from a friend's house or a friend has just left your house and he still has a high level of energy. You need ways to channel that energy positively—and prepare dinner for the family, at the same time.

As with the other household chores, the key to channeling that energy, and, by the way, helping your child develop independence, is let him help in the kitchen. There are many simple tasks, from tearing lettuce for the salad to mixing the pudding for dessert, that are time-consuming and give him a sense of self-confidence because he's doing a "real" job, and at the same time are skill builders.

If he's too young to help with the actual meal, or the menu is too complicated for a little helper, let your child mimic your actions. Give him a mixing bowl and spoon to play with; fill the sink with plastic containers to wash and rewash, or get out the play dough for him to make pretend cookies—these are all fun and satisfying for a young child.

Cooking with children is a lot of fun. They love the interesting textures of the ingredients. They're always ready with an opinion on the taste, touch, and smell of the ingredients—and, of course, of the final product. They usually throw themselves into the cooking process so intensely that it's a treat to watch.

And, the PROCESS is the most important part of any cooking experience with children. Here is where the real learning occurs. When you're cooking together, have your child participate as much as possible, from gathering the ingredients, to reading the recipe, to measuring, mixing, and serving.

When you cook with your child, it helps you be aware of just what he is learning. Because of this, you can better guide him. For example, you probably measure and mix pretty automatically. Yet, to your child, the very act of pouring water into a measuring cup to the correct level is math, small motor coordination, and science. (Remember, he still must learn, in this case through experience, that liquids take the shape of the container they are in.)

The recipes in this chapter and throughout the book are designed to be "read" by you and your child **TOGETHER**. Then, he will follow the sequential picture steps. Unless specifically designated as an adult activity (usually for safety reasons), he should be able to do or help you do each step in the recipe.

The skill-ful cook

In any cooking experience, children will be learning new vocabulary words for ingredients; descriptive words for tastes, textures, and smells; and action words for the operations they perform.

When you use together the recipes in this book, your child "reads" the pictures. He is learning the left to right progression necessary for reading books and developing other important prereading skills. He is learning sequence by following the steps in the recipe. He is practicing his recall skills and the ability to remember details, when he tells you how the applesauce, pudding, or bread was made, as you sit down to enjoy the finished product.

Your child can see the words for ingredients written on cans, boxes, and packages. He will often "read" them with the help of picture clues. You can pick out familiar letters in the word together.

Comparison is a very important skill for your child to develop. It will help him as he attempts to classify objects and ideas. The kitchen is full of opportunities for your child to practice comparing things. One of the best ways to show your child the meaning of comparatives is to show him something that is the opposite in meaning. When you compare the *hot* stove with *cold* ice cream, you help your child understand both concepts. Just think of all the examples you can provide through cooking!

- *fast/slow*—the beaters of a mixer
- *high/low*—the placement of dishes, pots, and pans on shelves
- *hard/soft*—pudding and a popsicle
- *heavy/light*—wooden and plastic bowls
- *full/empty*—measuring cups
- *thick/thin*—whipped cream and milk
- *liquid/solid*—make **–Sicles** on page 61 to demonstrate both concepts

Have your child "write" his own recipes, by making illustrations and dictating the words to you. He might want to create a whole cookbook of favorite recipes you have done together.

Believe it or not, children's literature and cooking go hand in hand. Remember Hansel and Gretel nibbling on the witch's gingerbread house or the gingerbread boy running away from everyone? Read those classics and then make a **Big Batch of Gingerbread** on page 63. (The recipe makes a lot of gingerbread, so it can be walls for a house, too.)

Here are some excellent books that can follow up your cooking experiences or lead you into the kitchen.

▶ Make the easy **Blender Applesauce** on page 62. For variety, make rosy applesauce by leaving the peels on the apples and putting the sauce through a food mill or colander. Then, read any or all of the following books: An Apple a Day by Judi Barrett; Apple Pigs by Ruth Orbach; Apples, a Bushel of Fun and Facts by Bernice Kohn.

▶ When you pick berries or buy them for making a pie, read Blueberries for Sal by Robert McCloskey. Let your child compare fresh berries with jam or jelly.

▶ After you've baked bread, read The Litttle Red Hen, a classic folk tale. Your child will love kneading the dough, so find a recipe you like and let him do this often. If you're not a baker, maybe you can visit a bakery.

▶ The Duchess Bakes a Cake by Virginia Kahl is the perfect book to read while enjoying a piece of a cake you've baked together. It's all about the importance of following directions. You'll both laugh at the adventures of the duchess who adds too large quantities to her cake recipe.

▶ Making scrambled eggs for a meal? Read Dr. Seuss' Green Eggs and Ham. If your child is an adventurous eater, add a little green food coloring to the eggs in the pan.

▶ The Popcorn Book by Tomie De Paola is full of information about this all-time favorite. There are several popcorn recipes at the end of the book. If it's winter, you might want to string some for the birds to eat.

▶ Making soup? Read Stone Soup by Marcia Brown, a classic folktale, or Mexicali Soup by Kathryn and Hayes Hitte. Talk about the ingredients as you cook. Have your child guess the ingredients in a soup or stew he has not helped you prepare.

▶ Cranberry Thanksgiving by Wende and Harry Devlin is a book to read at holiday time. There's a recipe for ''Grandma's Famous Cranberry Bread'' at the end of the book.

▶ Potato Pancakes All Around by Marilyn Hirsch talks about the traditional food prepared for another celebration—the Jewish holiday of Hanukkah. However, the delicious pancakes are fun to make any time of the year.

▶ If your family is a ''meat and POTATOES'' group, your child will enjoy hearing The Hungry Leprechaun by Mary Calhoun, an Irish folktale about the discovery of potatoes.

There are many more books that will relate to cooking. If you come to a cooking scene, while reading a book with your child, try to follow it up in your own kitchen.

-SICLES

JUICE AND MILK AND YOGURT-SICLES

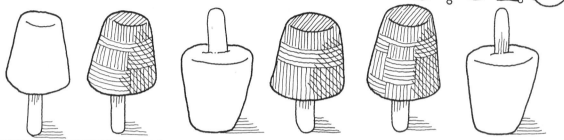

YOU'LL NEED:

5 oz. paper cups

plastic spoons- 1 per cup

 OR OR

fruit punch OR chocolate milk OR reconstituted orange juice

WHAT TO DO:

1. Choose 1 type of "-sicle" to make: orange, chocolate milk, or fruit punch.

2. Pour orange juice, chocolate milk, or fruit punch into cups.

3. Freeze about 1 hour and then add plastic spoon to the center.

spoons

5. Freeze until solid.

6. Peel away cup.

BLENDER APPLESAUCE

YOU'LL NEED:

   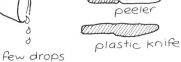 

6 apples   ½ cup honey   few drops of water   peeler   plastic knife   blender

WHAT TO DO:

 **1.** Peel the apples.

 **2.** Adult cuts each apple into 4 pieces.

 **3.** Put apples, honey, and a small amount of water into the blender.

 **4.** Blend until smooth. Enjoy!

YUM!

BIG BATCH OF GINGERBREAD

☆ THE GINGERBREAD BOY

YOU'LL NEED:

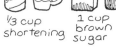 1/3 cup shortening

 1 cup brown sugar

 2/3 cup water

 1 1/2 cups molasses

 1/2 tsp. cinnamon

 1/2 tsp. nutmeg

  1/2 tsp. ginger

 1 tsp. salt

 2 tsp. baking soda

 spoon

   bowl   cookie sheet

  6 cups (or more) flour

raisins   nuts

WHAT TO DO:

1. Combine sugar, shortening, molasses.

2. Mix all dry ingredients together.

3. Add dry ingredients to moist ingredients. Mix.

4. Roll or pat out gingerbread people.

5. Decorate with raisins and nuts.

6. Bake at 350°F for 15 minutes on a greased cookie sheet.

Cooking and science

Cooking experiences help your child understand the growth process. They help him make connections—where foods come from, when they are available, the various parts of plants we use for food.

Some of the vegetables, like the carrot tops, will only make plant growth and not bear fruit. Seeds for new vegetables will grow from the greenery. This is an interesting life cycle for your child to observe. Talk about the needs of a plant. Read The Carrot Seed by Ruth Krauss.

By helping in the kitchen, your child will also observe how cooking changes foods through the addition of heat and cold. You can demonstrate very simple scientific principles just by making ice cubes and steam.

Make raisins with your child to show how heat changes such things as grapes. Point out that heat causes the water in the grapes to evaporate. Weigh a grape and then the raisin it becomes to show that something has been lost. Make the **Jumping Raisins** on page 66, a science recipe/experiment that will make everyone giggle.

TOGETHER

Growing plants helps your child learn about the origins of foods. By growing plants from parts of leftovers, he gets to see how the plant is used for food and where the seed came from to grow more of the same type of plant. Try some of the suggestions on the facing page.

Through cooking, your child will observe that single ingredients can be combined to make a completely different product, yet the product can never be broken down into its components, the ingredients, again. This is a science experiment that he will repeating in chemistry, later in school—with different ingredients, of course. You can show your child when you bake a cake how the eggs, flour, sugar, milk, and other ingredients make the cake, but cannot be separated from it afterwards.

Cooking with you helps your child understand many principles of experimentation. You try new ingredients in your recipes, plus add a little more of this or a little less of that. If you make a mistake, you see why it happened and can correct it next time. Many of the recipes you do together may not turn out as deliciously as you hoped. Talk about why they didn't work. This is an important part of science.

A cook's tools

The kitchen offers your child many opportunities to develop important physical skills. Look at the motor coordination he can develop using various kitchen tools. It will mean putting away your blender, electric juicer, and food processor for a while, but the results are well worth the time and effort.

▶ When your child uses a ROLLING PIN, he is gaining experience in forward, backward, and pressure motions. He can use the rolling pin to help you make dough or to crush crackers in a plastic bag for crusts. Make **Shortbread Puzzles** on page 69 together for a delicious, fun-filled experience with a rolling pin, as well as for a lesson in shapes. Your child can manage all the

GROW IT AGAIN!

Eat these vegetables and fruits and use different parts to grow new plants.

CITRUS TREE

Plant orange, grapefruit, or lemon seed 1/2" deep in soil.

It will take several weeks to sprout.

ONION

Find an onion that is already sprouted. Plant in soil.

TURNIP

Cut pointed end from turnip. Scoop out, leaving sides about 1/2" thick. Hang in a sunny window and keep filled with water.

AVOCADO

Set large end of avocado seed in jar of water, using 3 toothpicks. Sprout in partial sunlight. When the stem is about 4"-5" tall, plant in soil.

CARROT

Cut off top and trim off all leaves. Place in a layer of pebbles in a flat dish. Keep well-watered.

PINEAPPLE

Cut off the top and trim 3 rows of bottom leaves. Let dry for 3 days. Plant 1" deep in soil. Keep moist and sunny.

JUMPING RAISINS.

YOU'LL NEED:

 ½-1 lb. fresh green grapes

 dish or flat basket

paper towels

 club soda, seltzer, or lemon soda

 tall, clear glass   spoon

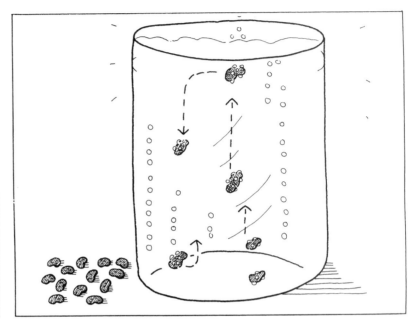

WHAT TO DO:

1.
Wash and dry with paper towels ½-1 lb. fresh green grapes.

2.
Place grapes in a dish or flat basket in a sunny, warm place.

3.
In nice weather, grapes will become raisins in a few days. If you place near a sunny window, it will take a little longer.

4.
When grapes have dried into raisins make

JUMPING RAISINS.....

5.
Pour club soda, seltzer, or lemon soda into a tall, clear glass. Add 4-6 raisins. Observe. Raisins will sink to the bottom, then slowly rise to the top. They will continue to jump up and down for several minutes.

6.
Wait until all the raisins settle to the bottom of the glass, then drink the soda. Get the raisins out with a spoon and eat!

preparation from the mixing and rolling to pricking and cutting. Try experimenting with different shapes of puzzles—round, square, and triangular ones. Have your child cut out special shapes with cookie cutters as part of the puzzle.

▶ Through SHAKING, your child develops hand, arm, and shoulder coordination, as well as concepts of up, down, left, and right. Shaking drinks and salad dressing gives him practice in this important skill. One fun recipe that calls for shaking is **Instant Pudding in a Bag** on page 70. This makes a special treat at celebrations since all the guests can participate in fixing it. It's a party game you can eat!

▶ Your child will feel very grown-up if he is given the opportunity to slice fruits and vegetables with a SERRATED, PLASTIC KNIFE (often used at picnics). He can practice the sawing motion by using his hand or his entire arm.

Make the **Singing Salad** together on page 71 for a musical, mathematical, summery supper. Your child gets to do lots of counting while preparing this recipe. First, he gets to peel, cut, core, chop, and use a melon baller. As a result, each whole fruit gets broken into parts. Then, he divides the parts into specific numbers as you sing the song together.

This recipe also can introduce your child to the skill of estimating. Have him try to figure out beforehand how much of each fruit you will need for the salad. Let him decide how big each piece should be and how many pieces can be cut from one whole fruit. Use the fruit, accordingly. Afterwards, see what is left over.

▶ When he uses a hand GRINDER, your child will feel the whole arm-shoulder movement. Grind vegetables to make soups or salads. Use the recipe on page 72 to make **Nut Butters**. Your child will be thrilled to see how one of his favorite foods gets from the shell into a spread. Try the nut butters with toppings, such as bacon or banana, or spread on lettuce. Put a nut butter into a stalk of celery, add raisins, and call it "ants on a log," a preschool favorite.

WARNING: Don't let children under four eat whole nuts. They are a prime cause of choking in young children.

▶ With a GRATER, your child can produce big and little curls with a downward motion of the wrist. Start off by having him grate soft foods like squash, raw potato, and cheese.

For a real treat, make **Sink and Float Dessert** on page 73. This is an excellent math activity as well. Besides measuring and counting the ingredients, your child can observe the number of layers in the final product. Talk about why some fruits sink and others float. If possible, relate this cooking experience to a similar activity in the bathtub (see page 37) or water play in the sink.

▶ Using a FORK, your child can mash cooked potatoes or hard boiled eggs with the pressure of his hand and finger muscles. He'll love making **Bird's Nest Egg Salad** on page 74. Once he has mastered this motion, he can use a real MASHER, which requires an up and down motion, to help you mash potatoes and vegetables.

▶ Fresh fruit juice tastes the best, and your child will be thrilled when the twisting motion of his hand and wrist as he works with a JUICER makes juice come out of an orange, lemon, or lime. Make citrus punch and sweeten with honey or, try the recipe for **Orange Sipper** on page 75 for a tangy treat. This fun way to create fresh orange juice can be used if your child is having difficulty with the juicer. It is also good for working off excess energy or a bad mood, as your child gets to push, punch, and press the half orange—and then, sip the delicious juice at the end.

▶ Your child may find that operating a HAND EGG BEATER is new experience since it involves a rotary wrist motion. Have him practice beating egg whites, whipped cream, and instant pudding. Mixing batter is a perfect activity to practice using an egg beater. Use the **pancake** recipe on page 76 and your child will become a creative chef.

Be sure to take a picture of your little chef with his special pancake, mount it on paper, and write the recipe with his additions underneath. This recipe may become a Sunday morning favorite with the whole family. In that case, consider making a pancake cookbook. Two good books to read, before or after the cooking experience, are The Perfect Pancake by Virginia Kahl and Pancakes, Pancakes by Eric Carle.

I Can Do It Myself Sandwiches on page 77 are both fun and creative and provide lots of practice in spreading. They also satisfy your child's need for independence. This recipe gives him a sense of control that recipes rarely do. Decision-making is such an important skill for children to develop so try to provide more than one or two choices. Usually, he will use the freedom in this recipe to make wise food choices and combinations (though they may not be your preferences). However, sometimes, he may come up with weird combinations or build ridiculous creations. Don't make him eat it if he doesn't want to. Remove him from the situation and talk about what he should be doing. Give him a chance to try again.

Math in the kitchen

There are math experiences for your child in every part of your kitchen—and you don't even have to be cooking.

▶ Start with unpacking your groceries. Have your child count the oranges in the sack or the eggs in a carton. Have him compare the sizes of cans and cartons. Then, ask him to sort the items—what goes in the refrigerator, the freezer, vegetable bin; on shelves in the cabinet; or under the sink. He can also classify items according to their use. *"What gets eaten at breakfast,*

SHORTBREAD PUZZLES

YOU'LL NEED:

 1/4 cup honey

 2 cups flour (white or whole wheat)

 1/2 cup (1 stick) butter or margarine

 plastic fork and knife

 bowl

 rolling pin

baking sheet

OPTIONAL:

 1 egg — 1 tsp. water — pastry brush

WHAT TO DO:

1. Place flour and butter in a bowl. Rub butter into flour.

2. Add enough honey to moisten into a stiff dough.

3. Use a rolling pin to roll out dough about 3/4" thick. Cut into a rectangular shape.

4. Prick all over with a fork.

5. Use a plastic knife to cut into large puzzle pieces.

6. Arrange on a baking sheet. If desired, brush with a mixture of 1 beaten egg and 1 tsp. water for a glossy look.

7. Bake in a 350°F oven for 20-30 minutes.

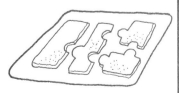

INSTANT PUDDING IN A BAG

YOU'LL NEED:

 1 ziplocking bag

 1 package instant pudding

 1 envelope dry milk

 1 3/4 cups water

 1 box ice cream cones

WHAT TO DO:

1. Measure dry milk needed to make 2 cups of liquid milk.

2. Add dry milk and 1 3/4 cups of water to ziplocking bag.

3. Empty pudding mix into bag. Zip it closed and shake well.

4. when thickened, open 1 corner of bag and squirt into cones.

SINGING SALAD

YOU'LL NEED:

 apples

 bananas

 blueberries

plastic knife

 melon (watermelon or canteloupe)

 paper cups

bowls

melon-baller

WHAT TO DO:

1. Prepare and set into separate bowls: melon balls, apple chunks, banana slices, blueberries.

2. For each individual serving, place the following in a cup and sing to the tune of "Ten Little Indians."

one little,
two little,
three little,
melon balls

four little,
five little,
six little
banana slices

eight little,
nine little,
apple chunks

ten little
blueberries!

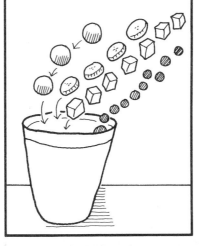

3. Vary the type of fruit used according to the seasons. Change the amounts- but, SING ALONG!

NUT BUTTERS

YOU'LL NEED:

 1 cup nuts

 blender

 OIL 2 Tblsp. salad oil

OPTIONAL: pinch of salt and/or sugar

WHAT TO DO:

1. Here is a list of nuts most commonly found in supermarkets:

 almond   filbert   pine

Brazil   macadamia   pistachio

cashew

chestnut   peanut   walnut

2. Talk about the color, shape, texture, and hardness of the nut shells. Try various ways of cracking the shells.....

 against each other.   with your hands.   with a rock.

with a hammer.   with a nut cracker.

Take out nut meat and grind into small pieces with a hand grinder.

3. TO MAKE **NUT BUTTERS**

1. Place 1 cup nuts in blender jar.

2. Add 1-2 Tblsp. salad oil. Blend until smooth or crunchy. Taste.

3. Add a pinch of salt and/or a pinch of sugar, if desired.

SINK AND FLOAT DESSERT

YOU'LL NEED:

 package of fruit-flavored gelatin

  ASSORTED FRUITS AND FILLINGS (see below)

spoon

clear bowl

water- according to directions

WHAT TO DO:

1. Prepare a package of fruit-flavored gelatin according to directions. If possible, prepare in a clear bowl.

2. When cool, but still liquidy, add some or all of the following:

 blueberries

mini-marshmallows

sliced banana

sliced peaches -OR- strawberries

grated coconut

 grated carrot

 chopped walnuts

crushed pineapple

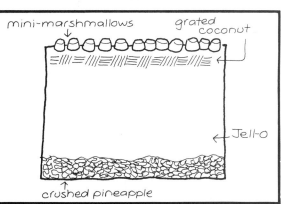 use canned pineapple - packed in its own juice.

3. Some of these things will float. Some will sink. Talk about why things sink or float.

Chill gelatin. Eat and see layers of fruit and gelatin. Make a chart about things that stay up (float) and things that go to the bottom (sink).

mini-marshmallows

grated coconut

Jell-O

crushed pineapple

BIRD'S NEST EGG SALAD

YOU'LL NEED:

 plastic strawberry boxes

 radishes, celery sticks, carrot sticks

 hard-boiled eggs

 lettuce OR chicory

 plastic fork and knife

 OPTIONAL: mayonnaise

WHAT TO DO:

1.
Line strawberry box with lettuce OR chicory.

2.
Peel hard-boiled eggs. Mash eggs with a fork or slice.

3.
Fill basket with egg salad or sliced eggs. Add assorted fresh vegetables.

sliced hard-boiled egg

radish

celery sticks

lettuce OR chicory

strawberry box "bird's nest"

ORANGE SIPPER

YOU'LL NEED:

 ½ orange (no seeds)

 1 drinking straw

 1 sandwich size zip locking plastic bag

WHAT TO DO:

 1. Place ½ orange in a plastic bag. Squeeze out most of the air.

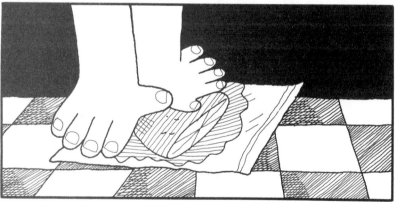

2. Seal plastic bag. Squeeze orange to get out juice.

 3. Open a corner slightly. Place straw inside and drink.

PANCAKES

YOU'LL NEED:

 1 egg

 ½ tsp. salt

 ½ tsp. baking soda

 1½ cups milk

 1½ cups flour

 3 Tblsp. oil or margarine

griddle

CREATIVE PART- see below

TOPPINGS- see below

 egg beater

WHAT TO DO:

1. BATTER

A. Beat milk and shortening (oil or melted margarine) together.

B. Add dry ingredients. stir until moistened

OR

instead of steps A and B, combine:

2 cups biscuit mix   and   2 eggs   and   1 cup milk   and   3 Tblsp. oil or melted margarine

---

2. CREATIVE PART

Add any or as many of the following:

 mashed banana

 raisins

 cinnamon

 chopped nuts

 chocolate chips

  ½ cup applesauce (use less water in recipe.)

  sliced fruit- strawberries, peaches, apples

---

3. TOPPINGS

A. Griddle the pancakes until golden brown.
☆ Add fruit to pancakes AFTER batter is poured in pan.

B. Serve as you wish with:

 syrup- maple or blueberry

 applesauce

 honey

 rolled up with fruit or cottage cheese

 spread with cream cheese or peanut butter

I CAN DO IT MYSELF SANDWICHES

YOU'LL NEED: -Washed and sliced vegetables and fruits-

cucumber   tomato   banana   apple   pear   carrot   zucchini

-Fillings-

peanut butter   whipped cream cheese   American cheese slices   mayonnaise   plastic knife

---

WHAT TO DO

1. Place a few sliced fruits or vegetables in small dishes.

2. Place 1 or 2 fillings in a dish.

3. Make sandwiches such as:

vegetable or fruit
↓

←filling

↑
vegetable or fruit

SANDWICH SNACKS

| outsides | Insides |

Make a chart.

lunch, dinner?" "What is used for cleaning?" "What goes on the table?"

▶ Unloading the dishwasher can mean classifying also—dishes, glassware, silverware, and so on.

▶ Stacking pots and pans helps your child experiment with size relationships. Give him a pot and the choice of three others which might fit inside. Talk about big, bigger, and biggest. Talk about inside, outside, on top of, and other directional words just so your child can hear them used in appropriate situations as he plays.

▶ If anyone in the family has ever been on a diet, you may have a simple scale around. This will give your child the opportunity to make comparisons by weight. Have him weigh anything and everything to see what is light, heavy, heavier, and so on.

▶ If you have a pie plate, you can introduce your child to the fun of fractions. Make several different paper "pies" for your child to serve—a blueberry pie may be three blue thirds; a chocolate pie may be two brown halves; a cherry pie may consist of red quarters. When you are cutting a real pie, always try to show your child how the pieces are part of the whole.

▶ Have your child use the kitchen timer to time all sorts of activities. "Does it take ten minutes to unpack the groceries? I'll set the timer and see." "Does it take five minutes to peel an orange? Let's find out."

▶ Here are some ideas that work particularly well with apples, but can be adapted to other fruits and vegetables.

■ Buy or pick in the fall a few apples of different types and sizes—McIntosh, Cortland, Rome, Greenings, or others.

■ Get to know each apple with your child. "What shape is it?" "Round?" "Long?" "What size is it?" "Small or big?" "Is it heavy or light?" "Find two apples that are about the same size." "The same weight."

■ Have your child see which apple is the fattest. Cut lengths of string to go around the widest part of each apple. Compare the lengths to see which apple is the fattest. Slice open an apple and have your child count the seeds.

The chef is an artist

When your child cuts up red, green, and yellow apples and makes a flower, using peanut butter and raisins for the center, he is creating a work of art. There are, however, many art materials in the kitchen that are not edible.

▶ Plastic locking bags can be used for a "nonmessy" fingerpainting experience. Partially fill a bag with ketchup, mustard, or paint. Lock tightly, making sure all of the air has been removed. By pressing with his fingers, your child can make lines and designs.

▶ Foam egg cartons make terrific glue or paint cups. Just cut them into as many sections as you need.

▶ Aluminum pie plates make lovely, shiny, hanging decorations. Trace a shape with a pencil on the bottom of a pie plate. Cut it out with scissors.

TOGETHER

Make a simple Balance and hang it in the kitchen. Have your child try various combinations of items to see what is heavier—two cherries or three cherries, three cherries or three walnuts, a cup of water or a cup of flour.

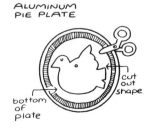

ALUMINUM PIE PLATE

cut out shape

bottom of plate

A BALANCE

YOU'LL NEED:

 1 wire coat hanger

 2 empty yogurt containers

string

 scissors

ruler

· SMALL MATERIALS ·

 acorns   pebbles   raisins

tape

dried fruits

WHAT TO DO:

tape →

 bend a wire hanger ↙

- Balance on door knob or edge of table top -

 YOGURT

 YOGURT

1.

Punch 3 holes evenly spaced around rims of the yogurt containers.

2.

Cut 6 pieces of string 1' in length. Tie each string firmly in each hole of yogurt containers. Then, join the 3 pieces together through 1 end of the hanger.

3.

Gather small materials like ACORNS, PEBBLES, and RAISINS. Hang balance on door knob or edge of table top. Your child can have a lot of fun experimenting with the balance.

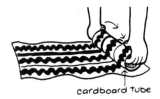
cardboard tube

TOGETHER

Foam egg cartons can be used to make many things—both artistic and useful. There are three suggestions on the facing page.

Color in the details with markers or paint. Hang with yarn.

▶ The kitchen offers many items for printing. Cookie cutters, sponges, and gadgets can be used.

▶ Reuse foam meat trays in printing, too. Wash them well in soapy water and dry. Have your child use a pencil with a broken point to draw a design or picture on the tray. Make sure he presses hard enough to make an indentation, but not hard enough to tear the tray. Brush or roll paint or printing ink over the tray. Place a piece of paper over the tray and have him rub gently. Peel off the paper and he'll have a lovely picture.

▶ Empty paper towel tubes also can be used for printing. Have your child glue yarn or string on a tube in a continuous design. Let it dry. Then, help him roll ink onto the yarn design. Finally, have him roll the tube on paper.

▶ Combine drinking straws with paint for an exciting effect. Place blobs of red, blue, and yellow paint on a piece of paper. Have your child blow a stream of air through the straw over the paint. The colors will spread and blend, making new colors. This is a good time to talk about how secondary colors are formed. Read Babar's Book of Colors by Jean de Brunhoff.

▶ For an artist's medium he can eat, make PEANUT BUTTER PLAY DOUGH with your child. *You'll need:* one cup of peanut butter, two or three tablespoons of honey, and ½ to ¾ cup of powdered milk. Stir the ingredients together in a bowl. Refrigerate for two hours. Have your child roll the mixture into balls. Then, he can mold it into his favorite shapes—and eat it when he is finished.

EGG CARTON IDEAS

YOU'LL NEED:

 brass paper fastener

 colored cellophane

 felt tip markers

2 pipe cleaners

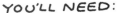  1 egg carton

scissors

large beans

WHAT TO DO:

1. LILIES

styrofoam egg carton section

(INSIDE) brass paper fastener

two ovals-cut from lid of styrofoam egg carton and attached with brass fastener.

Attach pipe cleaner stems

2. SUNGLASSES

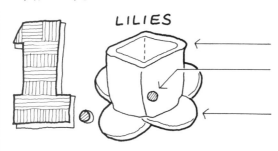

1. Cut away 2 sections of an egg carton.
2. Cut holes in bottoms of both sections and glue on pieces of cellophane to insides.
3. Attach pipe cleaners to fit over ears.

3. BEAN TOSS

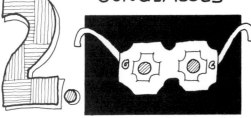

| 1 | 2 | 3 | 4 | 5 | 6 |
| 7 | 8 | 9 | 10 | 11 | 12 |

1. Use markers to write numerals in "holes" of an egg carton.
2. Call out a number. Player tosses a bean and tries to get it into that number's hole.
3. If player succeeds, he can keep the bean. See who can keep the most beans.

Parents' Snacking Guide

One of the problems we all have with spending so much time in the kitchen is that just being around food makes most people hungry. Children are no exception. They love to "snack." So, when your child says in between meals *"I'm hungry,"* here are some suggestions from expert, Janet Horowitz, that will provide him with good nutrition and fill his need for something extra to eat.

To encourage new and healthy foods, do not ask your child *"What do you want to eat?"* or *"Do you want a carrot?"* Just give him some or have him help prepare the snack. Your child is more apt to eat something new when it is in his hand or he is involved in making it.

Here are some tips for successful snacking.

■ Use a cookie cutter or knife to make interesting or unusual shapes out of such snacks as cheese, breads, and meat. Cut vegetables into circles, chunks, or sticks.

■ Serve snacks in small plastic bags so that your child can carry them around and eat when he is hungry.

■ Serve snacks in fun containers for added appeal. Try a clean toy boat or car.

■ Try a new location for snacktime.

■ Serve a dip with the raw vegetables and have a dunking party.

Children like to eat foods that they have prepared themselves. And, think of all the practice in motor skills the preparation involves. Consider some of the following—and, please remember that your child might like some of these snacks even if you don't. He has his own tastes and preferences and it's okay for them to be different than yours. Try something new together!

■ Spread tuna fish, peanut butter, or grated cheese, mixed with mayonnaise on celery sticks.

■ Serve fresh peas in the pod.

■ Dip carrot sticks in peanut butter.

■ Spread cream cheese on cucumber rounds.

■ Make your own "soda" with fruit juice and soda water.

■ Pop popcorn together. Bake some with cheese.

■ Mix cottage cheese with raisins and cinnamon. Put on toast and slide under the broiler, until bubbly.

■ Roll softened cream cheese in nuts or granola to form balls.

■ Dip pineapple chunks in honey.

■ Spread peanut butter on sliced apples.

■ Make "cracker jacks"—mix popcorn with honey, butter, and nuts. Bake.

■ Make a dip for raw vegetables—mix mayonnaise and ketchup or try a tuna and ricotta cheese mix or tuna and crushed pineapple.

Many doctors feel that the healthiest eating pattern for young children is five or six small meals a day. So, when your child wants to snack, he may be doing what is best and most natural for his growing body.

Cookbooks for Kids

Cooking with kids provides so much fun and learning that you will probably want to go beyond the recipes in this book. Here is a list of excellent cookbooks, chosen with preschoolers in mind by Mary Underhill.

■ Kids Are Natural Cooks by the Parent's Nursery School, Cambridge MA

■ Crunchy Bananas and Other Great Recipes Kids Can Cook by Barbara Wilma

■ Peter Rabbit's Natural Foods Cookbook by Arnold Dobrin

■ The Pooh Cookbook by Virginia H. Ellison

■ Cool Cooking - 16 Recipes without a Stove by Ester Hautzig

■ The A to Z No-Cook Cookbook by Felipe Rojas-Lombardi.

OUTSIDE CHORES 5

*O*utdoor explorer

A tree for all seasons

For the birds

*F*all

*W*inter

In the snow

*S*pring

April showers. . .

. . .Bring May flowers

*S*ummer

In the swim

Backyard neighbors

Outdoor Explorer

Your child can sharpen his senses—and his sense of wonder—as he explores his own backyard. Even if you live in an apartment and don't plant, weed, mow, rake leaves, or shovel snow from the driveway, take the time you would spend at these outdoor chores to find a park, vacant lot, or school yard nearby to explore with your child.

Nature is full of exciting things for your child to discover, and, each season, there are new discoveries to make. All he has to do is look, listen, touch, smell, and taste. He will be using his senses to learn in preschool and Kindergarten—so why not start now?

Read <u>What Do You See?</u> by Janina Domanski, a book which invites your child to explore the world. <u>The Other Way to Listen</u> by Lester Byrd Baylor talks to your child about how he can learn with his ears. The backyard and the park are wonderful places to practice listening skills.

As you do your work in the backyard, enthusiastically encourage his explorations. Don't always be the one to point out and explain, however. Let your child be the adventurer and look for "how come" himself.

Here are some suggestions from Early Childhood professor, Jean Stangl.

▶ Provide a hand lens (magnifying glass) to make investigating more interesting. Choose a lens that is safe, sturdy, and easy for your child to handle. A four-inch diameter magnifying glass, with an easy-to-grip handle, seems to work best with preschool children.

Using the lens, have your child observe the geometric shape of a spider's web or the veins on the underneath side of a leaf or count the spots on a ladybug or the legs on a grasshopper. Have him look for colors, shapes, similarities, and differences. After a rain, have him investigate an earthworm and its castings—little mounds of earth.

▶ Have your child explore the small world inside the space of a hula hoop or an old tire, placed on the grass or a dirt area. He will be amazed at the interesting plant and animal life existing there.

▶ Give him an old spoon to dig with in the dirt or let him use his hands. Together read <u>Earth</u> by Alfred Leutscher.

▶ Encourage him to turn over a rock and see what moves.

▶ Suggest that he explore the yard on his stomach. Have him stretch out flat and ask what he sees, hears, smells, and feels. Then, he can flip onto his back—never looking directly at the sun—and experience a totally different environment.

A tree for all seasons

Your child will discover new plants and animals and experience different sensations each season of the year. In addition, trees are never-ending, though often changing, fixtures in your yard (or the local park). Encourage your child to adopt one tree and "really get to know it." A special tree can provide hours of fun and learning; and be a special place to climb, hide, or just lie under and daydream.

According to Janet Horowitz, *"appreciation of trees—and all of nature—begins by getting to know them."* She suggests that you encourage your child to get close to his chosen tree, and do the following things:

■ hug it. *"How far do your arms go around it?"* Measure it with a string. Paste the string on paper. You can measure it year after year to see how it grows.

■ kiss it. Smell the bark, leaves, pine cones, flowers, and acorns.

■ explore it carefully with his eyes. Then, use a magnifying glass.

■ explore it carefully with his hands and feet. Have him close his eyes and feel the bark, leaves, twigs, and buds.

■ find out who lives in his tree. Point out that trees are homes for animals, birds, and insects. Look for nests— *"What is it made of? Who do you think built it?";* wet holes for mosquitoes, tree frogs, and polliwogs, and dry holes where you will find owls, woodpeckers, squirrels, and raccoons. Show your child some beehives that he can observe from far away.

Together find out as much as you can about your child's tree. Keep your findings in a book. Have your child draw a picture of his tree. Have him make a bark rubbing with paper and a wax crayon or candle stub. Paste in a leaf, twig, and seed. Take photos of your child next to or in the tree at each season. Label each season as you paste the picture in the book.

Your child can make a tree calendar by collecting buds and leaves from the tree at each season and pressing them between the pages of a book. When they are dry and flat, he can glue them to a simple drawing of the tree, one drawing for each season. Then, you can add calendar pages under each seasonal tree picture.

Have your child collect dead branches, twigs, and pieces of bark and make a wood sculpture, using glue to attach the pieces and a larger piece of wood for a base.

Also, with twigs from his tree, your child can make a picture frame by gluing four notched twigs to form a square or rectangle. Glue a piece of cardboard to the frame, and then a picture in the center.

Read two marvelous books, The Giving Tree by Shel Silverstein and The Dead Tree by Alvin Tresselt, that celebrate the lives and deaths of two special trees.

TOGETHER
You can take a large branch that has fallen from the tree and set it in a clay pot to make A Tree for All Seasons.

A TREE FOR ALL SEASONS

SETTING UP

sand

marbles

Set a tree branch into a clay pot with a brick or sand to hold it in place. The branch also can be set into a jar with marbles. If the jar is set near a window, the light will go right through the marbles, creating a beautiful effect.

JANUARY-FEBRUARY

Decorate your winter tree with snowflakes made from paper doilies, red and white bows, white dove cut-outs. Celebrate the Oriental New Year with accordion-folded fans and paper lanterns. Hang heart-shaped cookies.

① cut ② tape→

PAPER LANTERNS

MARCH-APRIL-MAY

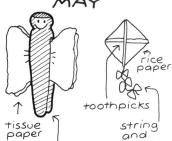

tissue paper

rice paper

toothpicks

clothespin
BUTTERFLY

string and paper
KITE

Green is a springtime color and the color of the St. Patrick's Day shamrock. Cut shamrocks from green paper. Make an Easter tree by adding blown-out eggs that are dyed pastel colors or covered with tissue paper. Add clothespin and tissue paper butterflies, egg carton tulips and caterpillars, and toothpick kites.

JUNE-JULY-AUGUST

Show your colors in summer with red, white, and blue paper chains and flowers.

To make the flowers- cut strips of 12"x 14" red, white, and blue tissue paper and place the 3 strips together. Gather them with fingers down the center and twist a pipe cleaner on to hold it. Add a red, white, and blue paper chain. Cut out large circles and color as suns and beach balls.

SEPTEMBER-OCTOBER

Decorate a tree with a photograph of your child. Fold red and orange paper in half and cut apple and pumpkin shapes. Collect real fall leaves and use them as models to cut out paper ones. Hang on tree.

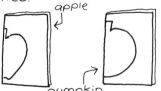

apple
pumpkin

NOVEMBER-DECEMBER

1. Tape on toothpicks.
a. X
3. Tape and decorate.
TEPEE

TURKEY
1. Trace hand.
a. Trim. Draw in features.

Include Thanksgiving, Hanukkah, and Christmas on your holiday tree. Make hand-print turkeys, mini-tepees, and walnut shell ships for Thanksgiving. Roll pinecones in glue and then into glitter. Hang with bright yarn. Cut out 5 and 6 pointed stars. Add tinsel for a sparkling effect. Twist 1 red and 1 white fuzzy pipe cleaner together for a candy cane.

For the birds

Birds are interesting for your child to observe all year round. Serious bird watching should be done very early in the morning. Both you and your child should wear neutral colors. Talk to your child beforehand about how to be very quiet. Explain that you will see different birds at different seasons. Have your child draw pictures of each kind of bird he sees. If you have binoculars, he can look at the different kinds of feathers and markings on each bird, as well as the distinctive beaks. Encourage him to make observations using questions like the following.

■ *"Do all birds fly the same way?"*
■ *"How do they move on the ground?"*
■ *"What kinds of noises do they make?"*
■ *"Do they carry anything in their beaks?"*

Here are some seasonal activities for young bird lovers.

▶ In the FALL, watch birds migrating. *"Do they fly alone or in groups?"* *"Where do you think they are going?"*

▶ In the late FALL and WINTER, birds often have a hard time finding enough food to eat. (In the winter, a small bird may eat one third of its weight each day to keep warm and full of energy.) So hang home–made bird feeders outside. Stuff pine cones with melted suet or bacon grease which has been mixed with peanut butter, and roll them in birdseed. Fill empty orange or grapefruit halves with birdseed and hang on trees with string. Use a needle and thread to string bits of suet, orange sections, cranberries, popcorn, and even chunks of doughnuts, and hang them around bushes. (If your child is sick and must stay in bed, a birdfeeder hung right outside his window can provide hours of entertainment.)

▶ In the SPRING, put out colorful, short (three-to-five inch) pieces of yarn for the birds to use in building their nests. Hang them on a tree branch or stuff them in an mesh onion bag. Have your child see if he can spot the yarn in birds' nests around the neighborhood.

▶ In the SUMMER, make a birdbath for your backyard. Use a garbage can lid, a pie tin, or other shallow, unbreakable container. Put it in a shady place off the ground and keep it filled with water. Your local birds will appreciate your thoughtfulness.

▶ From MIDSUMMER to early FALL is the best time for feather collecting. Pour boiling water over the ones found by your child to clean them before using. Have him study them under a magnifying glass. *"Can you find different colors, shapes, and sizes?"* If he is finding quite a few, draw on paper and cut out a large, simple bird shape. Hang it on the wall and have your child glue on the feathers as he finds them. Soon, he will have a feathered friend in his room!

Fall

Fall brings to mind raking leaves, gusty winds, lengthening shadows, migrating birds—and also, lots of learning for young children.

Fall is a good time for your child to become a collector—of fallen leaves, acorns, seed pods, horse chestnuts, sunflower seeds, and feathers. He can use his collections for a myriad of learning experiences.

▶ Put out a **Balance Scale** (instructions for making one can be found on page 79) for your child to compare the relative weights of the things he finds. *"Which is heavier, an acorn or a feather?" "Which is lighter, one or two acorns?"*

▶ Provide an egg carton for your child to use for sorting his treasures. Classifying is a very important thinking skill.

▶ An egg carton can also be used as a place to count when you add some seeds. See if your child can put one seed in the first section, two in the next, and so on.

▶ You can make a simple matching shape game by tracing the outlines of a few fall objects like leaves and acorns onto the bottom of a shirt box. Have your child match the item to its outline on the box. Then, he can look around the yard for other items that are the same shape.

½ egg carton
SAMPLES

▶ Keep a box with wind testers in it—feathers, crepe paper streamers, yarn, and old scarves—for your child to use as a cape on a windy day.

▶ Have your child find a few leaves of the same type that range from small to large. Challenge him to arrange them in size order.

▶ Keep a thermometer in a convenient place outside and record the temperature each day. Fall is a good time to discuss the concepts of warm and cool in relation to how it feels each day.

▶ The fall is an excellent time to talk with your child about shadows (which are getting longer each day). *"Do only people make shadows?"* Have your child observe many objects including his tree. He might want to measure the shadow made by his tree every few days at the same time each day. *"Is it growing longer?"* Teach your child how to play shadow tag—the person who is "it" must step on the other players' shadows. Read the book, <u>Shadows, Here, There, and Everywhere</u> by Ron and Nancy Goor.

You can make a simple shadow clock in your backyard with a pencil and a paper plate. Insert the pencil halfway through the center of the plate. Stick the pencil into the ground. It will make a shadow on the plate. Mark the shadow with another pencil; come back an hour later and see if the shadow has moved.

▶ If you live somewhere that fall leaves turn brilliant colors and fall to the ground, your child is in luck. There are many things he can do with those fallen leaves that are such a chore for you to rake. After he has had his fill of jumping in them and messing around, he will probably want to know why the leaves change color. You can show him by taking a spinach leaf from the kitchen and removing its chlorophyll with alcohol. (The leaf will turn yellow.)

TOGETHER

Besides pressing, printing, and making rubbings with leaves, you may want to try some of the more unusual projects on the next page.

Point out that the green just covers the autumn colors of the leaves all summer, until it gets cooler and not so sunny.

▶ If your child is able to gather lots of seeds outside, he can use them for art projects as well as for counting and sorting.

▶ He can make a mosaic by gluing seeds in designs onto a piece of cardboard.

▶ He can make jewelry by soaking pumpkin, squash, or other flat seeds in warm water for one hour. Then, he can string them on heavy thread with a sharp needle. (This is for five- and six-year-olds.)

▶ He can make a flower by cutting a two-inch circle from cardboard and stapling it to a plastic straw, cut in half. He can glue seeds to the cardboard to create the petals.

▶ If your child finds berries in the backyard, he can crush them with a wooden spoon and use the juices to paint pictures. (Add a little vinegar to avoid mold.) He can use paintbrushes, stick pens, or even a bird's feather with the end cut to a point.

▶ Encourage your child to preserve the smells of the season by making a potpourri. Have him collect flower petals and their leaves—roses, violets, jasmine, narcissus—and herbs—basil, sage, lavender, thyme. Help him dry his collection on paper towels in an airy, dry place, out of the sunlight. When dry, mix in a bowl with one teaspoon of orrisroot to each pint of petals. Add spices, like cloves, cinnamon, or allspice, if you wish. Put the mixture in a tightly covered jar for six weeks. Then, help him make sachets or keep the mixture in baskets around the house.

Fall is a wonderful time to be outside. While you are getting the yard ready for winter, your child can be appreciating the beauty of nature and creating some beautiful things on his own.

When you're through with your projects, sit with your child under a colorful tree or in a pile of leaves and read. Here are some suggestions: <u>Marmalade's Yellow Leaf</u> by Cindy Wheeler; <u>Autumn Story</u> by Jill Barklem; <u>All for Fall</u> by Ethel and Leonard Kessler; <u>Fall Is Here</u> by Jane Monecure; and <u>Say It!</u> by Charlotte Zolotow. This is truly a season to cherish each year.

POTPOURRI

LEAVES

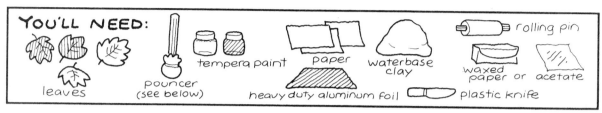

YOU'LL NEED:

leaves

pouncer (see below)

tempera paint

paper

waterbase clay

rolling pin

waxed paper or acetate

heavy duty aluminum foil

plastic knife

WHAT TO DO: SILHOUETTES

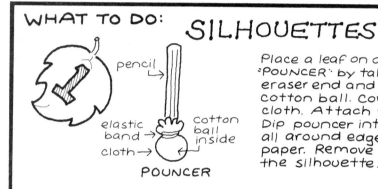

pencil

elastic band

cotton ball inside

cloth

POUNCER

Place a leaf on a sheet of paper. Make a "POUNCER" by taking a pencil with an eraser end and padding the end with a cotton ball. Cover with a square of cloth. Attach with an elastic band. Dip pouncer into thick paint and pat all around edges of leaf and onto paper. Remove leaf and see the silhouette!

FOIL PRINTS

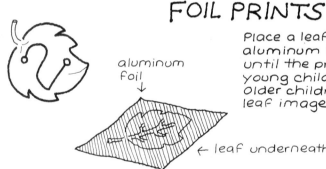

aluminum foil

← leaf underneath foil

Place a leaf under a piece of heavy duty aluminum foil. Press and rub the foil until the print of the leaf appears. For young children, this part is fun enough. Older children may want to cut out leaf images and mount on cardboard.

LEAF TILES

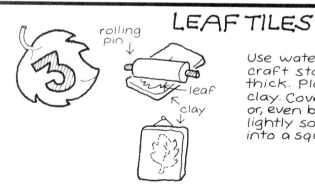

rolling pin

leaf

clay

Use waterbase clay (available at art and craft stores). Roll clay to about ½" thick. Place a deeply veined leaf on the clay. Cover with a piece of waxed paper or, even better, acetate. Roll again lightly so that leaf prints into clay. Cut into a square. Let it dry.

Winter

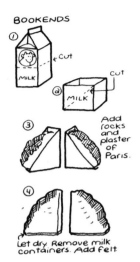

BOOKENDS

① Cut

MILK

② Cut

MILK

③ Add rocks and plaster of Paris.

④ Let dry. Remove milk containers. Add felt.

TOGETHER

With smaller stones and pebbles, make Rock People. You can also make animal rocks and place them in cages, made of cutout cardboard boxes.

Your child collects leaves in the fall, flowers in spring, shells in the summer; but, what about winter? Treasures do lie hidden in your yard in winter—rocks, stones, and pebbles. Sometimes, these treasures are truly buried—under the snow; so they are even more fun to find.

What can your child do with his finds?

▶ He can sort them, classify them, weigh them, line them up in order of size—all the time practicing premath skills.

▶ He can examine them with a magnifying glass to see the different colors and even shapes inside. Read Rock Collecting by Rita Gams.

▶ He can shine pebbles by rubbing them with a little baby oil, coating them with clear varnish, or tumbling them until they are smooth and shiny. To tumble stones, fill a one-pound coffee can about one third full of rough pebbles or stones. Fill the can with water. Secure the top of the can. Then, have your child shake the can. This is a slow process; it will take a few weeks of shaking. Place the can somewhere your child will see it often—and give it a few shakes.

▶ Large rocks can be used to make paperweights or bookends. To make a PAPERWEIGHT, help your child find a smooth stone, and then, let your child paint it with acrylics or enamel paints. Spray it with clear polyurethane to keep it shiny and easy to clean. Glue a piece of felt to the bottom to keep the paperweight from scratching furniture.

To make BOOKENDS, have your child find two large rocks with similar shapes. Take two quart paper milk or juice containers and cut them in half. Take the bottom half of each one and cut it on the diagonal. Tilt these pieces so that the bottom sides are up. Now, fill them with diluted plaster of paris. Put one rock in each carton, so that the rock is mostly showing through the plaster. Let them dry. Remove the containers and glue felt to the bottom of each to make a handsome set of bookends.

In the snow

You may not spend a lot of time outside doing chores during the winter, but someone has to plow the driveway—and, while your child will want to help you, there are many more fun and productive ways he can experience the frosty natural world.

▶ Help your child build a snowman just about his own size. Then, he can dress the snowman in his own sweater, scarf, and hat.

▶ Encourage him to make snow shapes. With pine needles, sticks, bark, and small stones, he can create a "snow animal zoo."

▶ Put out various-sized boxes for your child to pack with snow. When he turns the boxes upside down, he can build igloos, houses, or castles.

▶ Make a maze with your child. Mark a starting place; then, let him walk through the snow in all different directions to a finish line. See if you or another child can get through the maze.

▶ With two children in snowsuits, have knee races in the snow. Let children

ROCK PEOPLE

YOU'LL NEED:

 small rounded rocks

white glue

acrylic paints and paintbrushes – or –

felt tip markers

WHAT TO DO:

1. Pile 2 or 3 rocks together to make a figure. Glue well and let dry.

2. Use paints or markers to add features.

3. Make roads and rock houses for a town where the rock people can live.

see who "runs faster" through the snow on his knees.

▶ Put diluted food coloring in empty, thoroughly washed-out spray bottles. Your child can spray colors on the ground to make designs in the clean, white snow.

▶ Make three snowballs. Let your child see you hide a treat—tiny plastic toy, bell, or wrapped candy—in one snowball. While he is watching, move the snowballs around. Have him guess in which snowball the treat is hidden. Then, let him hide the treat for you to find.

Back inside, by the warmth of the fire or sipping hot chocolate, read together these books about winter: A Snowy Day by Ezra Jack Keats; Baby Bear and the Long Sleep by Andrew Ward; The Mitten by Alvin Tresselt; The Winter Wedding by Robert Welber; Marmalade's Snowy Day by Cindy Wheeler; A Walk on a Snowy Night by Judy Delton.

▶ Watch the snowflakes together as they fall. Talk about the pretty shapes that stick to the window pane. Your child can make MAGIC SNOWFLAKES with a little help from you. *You'll need:* a square sheet of paper folded in half, top to bottom, then folded at the edges, and finally folded in half once more. Let your child cut pieces from the folded sheet at random. Then open the folded and cut paper to reveal a snowflake! Now, comes the magic. Place the snowflake under a sheet of typing paper. Have your child rub the paper with the side of a crayon and the snowflake will appear, again.

HOW TO MAKE AND FOLD A SNOWFLAKE

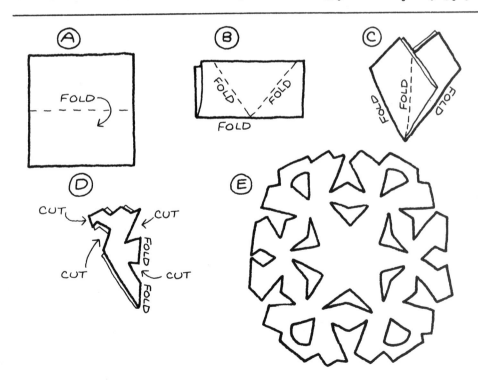

Spring

April showers. . .

Spring is a time for beautiful flowers, but as the song says, it is also a time for a lot of rain in many areas. Don't think about what you can't do because it's raining outside; instead be thankful for all of the wonderful learning experiences wet weather can provide for your child.

Your child can experience rain through his senses. He can observe the drops and puddles that form; he can listen to the sounds that raindrops make when they hit different objects; he can smell the special odors of a rainy day; he can even taste the rain if he sticks out his tongue.

Use the rain to help your child learn about colors. Have him make a painting with watercolors on a paper plate. Put the plate out in the rain for a minute or two. The colors will run together and you can talk about the designs they make and the new colors that are created.

What better time than after a spring rain to introduce your child to the joys of MUD! Mud was probably one of the earliest media for creative art, and is delightful just for squeezing, squishing, rolling, and pounding that can be done with it. Through soothing mud play, nature provides the perfect outlet for all that energy pent up sitting inside on a rainy day. Please, don't let your child miss out on the sheer pleasure of walking barefoot in soft, cool, gushy mud! Think of all the marvelous, descriptive words he can learn!

While you are cleaning up after a rain, your child can be building roads, houses, and mountains in your backyard. Clay-type soils hold their shape well when mixed with water, and they will dry hard. However, if your soil does not hold its shape, and you want to try some of the following activities with your child, you can add flour, wallpaper paste, or even liquid glue to a few cups of mud to give it the right consistency.

▶ Show your child how to roll mud into ropes. He can use them to make shapes, numbers, and letters.

▶ Encourage your child to roll some mud out like cookie dough, using a rolling pin or wooden dowel. He can then create shapes with old cookie cutters or a plastic knife.

▶ Ice cream sticks can be used to create numbers, shapes, letters, and designs in wet mud.

▶ If you just can't stand the idea of your child getting full of mud—or, if your child doesn't like the feel of mud oozing through his fingers—try mud fingerpainting. Let your child put a few spoonfuls of soil in a plastic locking bag. Slowly, add water and squeeze to mix. Now, zip up the bag and place on a flat surface. Your child can push his fingers around and make designs without getting even his hands dirty!

Mud and water in plastic locking bag

...Bring May flowers

It's spring! Time to get back into the yard and plant your garden. Your child will be a most enthusiastic gardener. Create a GARDEN HELPER KIT and he will really feel like a pro. *You'll need:* some strong plastic or metal garden tools—an old spoon and fork will work nicely; seed packets; a small watering can; a straw hat; a red work handkerchief; and a box or child-sized wheelbarrow to carry everything around.

Let your child help you plan the garden or at least part of it. He may want to buy some seeds of his own. The Gurney Seed Company (Yankton, South Dakota 57079) offers a child's seed packet for a penny that holds a mixture of 100 types of vegetable and flower seeds. He can drop his seeds, cover them with soil, water them, and then harvest his vegetables or flowers eventually.

Most seeds take seven to fourteen days to sprout, some even longer. Flower seeds, like nasturiums, sprout quickly, as do beans and peas. Your child will wonder what happens to his seeds after he plants them in the ground. Sandwich some seeds between the sides of a plastic, see-through glass and some damp paper towels. This will let him see what happens to a seed that is planted in the dirt. Egg cartons make excellent indoor planters with a few seeds and a thin layer of dirt in each section. For other indoor plant ideas, read How to Grow a Jelly Glass Farm by Kathy Mondry and Joe Toto. Share with your child The Little Seed by Eric Carle and The Carrot Seed by Ruth Krauss.

Some plants root in water. Take cuttings from easy-to-root plants, like coleus, ivy, and geranium, and place them in a clear, plastic glass, half full with water. They should start to root within a week. As the roots grow, have your child count them. Help him look for primary and secondary roots.

Once shoots have begun to appear in the garden or you have transplanted the cuttings, your child will want to check every day for new growth. He can measure stems and count leaves once a week. Together read How My Garden Grew by Anne and Harlow Rockwell.

Weeding is one chore you wish you could assign to your little helper, but, unfortunately, it's very difficult for enthusiastic young (and, sometimes, old) gardeners to tell the difference between weeds and young vegetables or flowers. Instead, assign him his own weed-infested area outside the garden.

Through gardening, your child is developing many skills and concepts. He is practicing his small motor skills, as he plants, waters, and weeds. He is learning to make a plan and carry it out. He is learning patience and how to deal with disappointment—when all his plants don't grow. He is learning what makes plants grow, where some of our food comes from, and how it gets from a seed packet to the table.

Summer

In the swim

You probably spend a great deal of time outdoors in the summer; I move as many chores as possible outside; then I can enjoy the weather and be with my daughter, too.

One problem we all have in the summer is how to beat the heat. Water play is the answer for your child. Put out a big tub of soapy water and a lot of empty plastic containers and picnic plates and utensils, and give your child the job of washing them. Fill a bucket with water and give your child a small or medium-sized paintbrush and have him paint the house or the sidewalk or the driveway. Have fun together dashing through the sprinklers.

If you have a wading pool, you can give your child a headstart on swimming. Here are some excellent suggestions from Ellen Javernick, a Colorado preschool teacher. The object of these games is for your child to be comfortable getting his face wet. If you've already tried some of the bathtub games on page 36, play them now in the pool to get your child used to the new environment. Then, try some of these more active games.

▶ Play "Ring around the Rosie" and "Jack in the Box," splashing as much as possible.

▶ "Run and Fall Down" Hold your child's hand and run across the pool. Have someone else call out "All fall down." Through this game, you can show your child how to use his hands to catch himself when he falls in the water by accident.

▶ "Catch" In this game, you hope your child won't catch the ball! Use a beach ball to throw back and forth. When he does miss and the ball hits the water, it will give him a pretty good splash—he'll hardly notice because he's concentrating on catching.

▶ "Humpty Dumpty" Say the rhyme as your child sits on the edge of the pool. Encourage him to "have a great fall" at the appropriate time.

▶ "Alligator" Show your child how to be an alligator by putting his hands on the bottom and stretching out his legs for a tail. Have the alligator crawl backwards and forwards. Let him "bite" your fingers. This is an important first position for your child because it encourages him to become horizontal in the water without having to get his face wet.

▶ "Submarine" Have your child be a submarine moving through the water, alligator position, until you call "Submarine," and he submerges.

▶ "Take a Deep Breath" To the tune of "London Bridge," sing "Take a deep breath, down you go, down you go, down you go. Take a deep breath, down you go, my good swimmer." Have your child act out the words as you sing.

▶ "Motor Boat" Use the rhyme "Motorboat, motorboat, go so slow." Hold hands and walk around in a circle in the water. "Motorboat, motorboat, goes so fast." Run in a circle. "Motorboat, motorboat, runs out of gas." Fall down in the water.

▶ "Treasure Hunt" "Hide" coins or poker chips on the bottom of the pool and let your child search for the treasure and then bring it to the surface.

Some children are "turtles." They just don't like getting their faces wet. If you have a turtle—he probably hates shampoos and showers, too, go slowly. Goggles or masks often help these children overcome their fears.

On the other hand, if you have a fish, who loves these games and is ready really to swim, you can can teach him a few of the basics before you need to be in deep water.

▶ "Tummy Float" Sit in the pool and have your child be an alligator on your knees. In this, as in everything else, let your child hold you. Then, he's in control, and can let go when he's ready. Ask him to put his face in the water and blow bubbles. When he can put his face in comfortably, he can let go of your knees and just float. Soon, he'll be able to start the float himself from an alligator position on the bottom.

▶ "Tummy Float with Kick" Don't expect a straight-legged flutter from your child at first. His muscles and coordination are not developed enough for this. The younger the child, the more it will look as though his legs are just crawling through the water.

Before getting into the water, have your child practice kicking while sitting on a chair. Hold his feet and kick for him. Emphasize "kicking feet." If you say *"kick your legs,"* you'll end up with a rocker, who kicks from the hip.

Of course, whenever and wherever you're in the water with your child, always emphasize water safety. *"Never, never swim alone"* is the one rule he must learn from the start.

Backyard neighbors

Summer is the perfect season for your child to investigate the animals, birds, and insects that live in his backyard. Small creatures fascinate young children—they want to examine them, feed them, and take care of them.

Your child can learn so much from experiences with these small creatures (though you may have to overcome some uneasiness about handling them).

Your child can hunt for ants, caterpillars, moths, butterflies, spiders, crickets, earthworms (especially after a rain), and frogs, turtles, and tadpoles—if you live near a pond or stream. First, however, you must teach him how to handle each creature carefully and gently. Too often, young children destroy insects and small animals by accident because of poor small muscle control or because they have seen others do it. Remind your child that little creatures are frightened of loud noises and big people so he must be especially quiet and careful when he observes them.

TOGETHER

Make a Bug Keeper and Net to help your child with his animal and insect studies. Both of these projects have been adapted from an excellent book, Teachables from Trashables by Toys 'N Things Press.

BUG KEEPER AND NET

BUG KEEPER

wire twister →

old, clean nylon stocking

bottom half of bleach bottle

YOU'LL NEED:

- old, clean bleach bottle
- old, clean nylon stocking
- wire twister
- dirt, grass, and twigs
- scissors or craft knife. ADULT USE ONLY

WHAT TO DO:

1. Cut away top of bleach bottle.
2. Cut windows around bottle.
3. Pull stocking over whole bottle.
4. To put bug in, just unfasten the top.
5. Add some dirt, grass, and twigs with leaves on bottom of the bottle.

NET

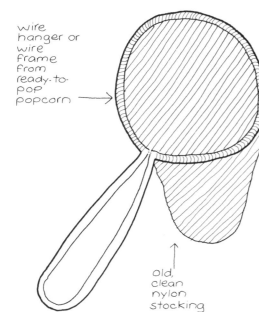

wire hanger or wire frame from ready-to-pop popcorn →

old, clean nylon stocking

YOU'LL NEED:

- wire clothes hanger or a frame from ready-to-pop popcorn with aluminum foil and pan removed
- nylon stocking
- needle and thread

WHAT TO DO:

1. Use frame or bend hanger into net shape.

2. Stretch stocking over frame and sew on tightly next to metal frame. Shorten to length desired and tie.

3. Catch insects or fish.

Encourage your child to study the creatures he finds with a hand lens or magnifying glass. Ask him questions such as the following.

■ "What does the creature look like?" "What color is it?" "How many legs does it have?" "Can you see its mouth?" "What else does it remind you of?"

■ "Where do you think this creature lives?" "Where did you find it?"

■ "What do you think it eats?" "Grass, cereal, insects?"

■ "How does it move?" "Try to move the same way."

■ "Listen. What sounds does it make?" "Make the same sounds."

Read books to help your child find out more about the little creatures he locates. Try Pets in a Jar by Seymour Simon and The Very Hungry Caterpillar by Eric Carle. The Snail's Spell by Joanne Ryder tells the story of a child who becomes like a snail to get to know the inhabitants of the garden.

If your child has caught a small creature in his net or is observing an insect in his Bug Keeper, talk about the need to release small animals unharmed. (The best place to do so is usually where you found them.)

While it is not a good idea for your child to keep most of the small creatures he finds, ants and earthworms can do very well in a man-made environment, and they are very interesting to observe over time.

TOGETHER

Construct a Home-made Ant Farm; then, have your child look for an ant hill in the backyard.

If you are making an ant farm with your child, you may scoop up some white material, along with the dirt, while collecting insects. (These "white things" are ant eggs.) Ants start out as eggs, become larvae—fat, little, white worms—then pupae—some will spin cocoons, like butterflies, and finally ants. Your child may be able to observe some of these stages in his ant farm. If your child gets the "queen" ant in his farm, he will soon have an active community. He can observe the ants cleaning, hunting for food, and even communicating with each other.

Ask your child questions about his little pets.

■ "What do they need to live?" Food? Water? Air? "How do they get these things?"

■ "What do they do all day?" "Do they sleep?"

■ "What do you think they 'say' to each other?"

■ "Where do they prefer living?" "In a Jar? Outside in your yard?"

HOMEMADE ANT FARM

YOU'LL NEED:

 1 quart mason jar with a removable lid insert

 strands of grass or leaves

twig

 small shovel

 fine window screen patch

scissors

  1/2" square piece of sponge   active ant hill

black construction paper

ASSORTED FOOD FOR ANTS: wheat germ, grass seed, chopped meat, dead bugs, sugar, bread, cooked bacon

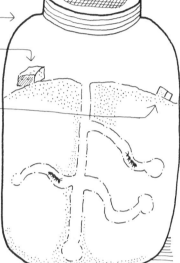

Screen

1 quart mason jar with removable lid insert

moist sponge

Food

 black construction paper ↓

WHAT TO DO:

 1. Using the jar lid insert, trace and cut a piece of screen to use inside of the jar lid rim. Discard the insert, and fit the screen into the lid in its place.

 2. Search for an ant hill. Fill the mason jar 2/3's of the way up with dirt and ants from the hill. Add a few leaves, grass strands, and twigs to the ants' new home.

 3. Saturate sponge with water and place it on top of the soil in the jar. Make sure the sponge is always moist as the ants will die if their home is allowed to dry out.

 4. Sprinkle 1 or more of the following items on top of the soil regularly: wheat germ, grass seeds, chopped meat, sugar, dead bugs, and cooked bacon. A sugar cube is a good food supply with which to start.

 5. Screw on the jar lid, making sure that the screen is firmly in place. Be careful not to shake the jar too much or you will destroy the "rooms" that the ants have created.

 6. When you are not watching the ants, tape a piece of black construction paper around the jar, to make the dark environment to which the ants are accustomed.

PLACES TO GO 6

Safe going

To the mall

Before shopping

While you shop

After you get home

To the supermarket

To the library

To the doctor

Places you wait

To the bank

To the office

Before the visit

During the visit

After the visit

Safe Going

Besides the many things you have to do around the house, you have many places to go outside the home, and often, your child goes with you. These excursions—to the supermarket, a mall or department store, the library, the doctor or dentist, on special occasions to your place of business—can be wonderful learning experiences for your child. A little preparation on your part can turn a potential nightmare into a really enriching and pleasant experience.

My most important concern when I take my preschooler anywhere is safety. With all of the stories about kidnapped children, I used to be hesitant to take her with me even to do errands; but, leaving her home was impractical, as well as a waste of valuable learning experiences and time together.

I was grateful to read an article by Dr. Sally Bing, of the University of Maryland-Eastern Shore, that offered concrete suggestions for handling the problem and my fears. She points out that children are very trusting and we don't want them to lose this trust and innocence. On the other hand, we must teach them not to trust persons who might harm them; and we parents must be able to deal with potentially dangerous situations. Here are Dr. Bing's suggestions.

▶ Read to your child about friends and strangers. Never Talk to Strangers by Irma Joyce is a colorful book, involving a little boy and a series of animal friends and strangers. This story helps your child understand what a stranger is without unduly scaring him. It suggests acceptable behavior with both friends and strangers.

▶ Teach your child never to accept a gift or go anywhere with a person without first checking it out with you to see if it is okay. This rule is particularly helpful to the young child who does not fully understand what is meant by the word "stranger."

▶ Teach your child to yell loudly for help if a person approaches and persists in talking to him and demanding that he go with him. Many kidnappings take place silently without anyone being aware of what is happening.

▶ Role play meeting friends and strangers and what to do in each situation. Remember that you are not trying to make your child fear people he does not know. Rather, you want to teach him to ask permission before accepting something or going with another person.

▶ Take your child with you whenever you leave the car. Leaving a child alone in a car is an invitation to trouble. It takes no time at all to coax a young child into unlocking a car door.

▶ Stay with your child when he wishes to stop and look at something in a store, even though it increases your shopping time. Children have been known to disappear when they were only an aisle away from their parents.

▶ Always, accompany your child to the restroom in a public place. Little boys, as well as girls, can go with their mothers to the ladies' restroom, and, if necessary, girls can accompany their fathers. NEVER send a child alone.

► If your child should disappear in a store, ask the store personnel to close all the exits immediately and search the store. Kidnappers can swiftly change a child's appearance to get out of exits when people "are on the lookout" for a specific person.

► Take advantage of fingerprinting and identification programs offered by local civic groups and/or the police department. Should anything happen, there will be positive identification records of your child.

► Keep an eye out for all children, not just your own. How many times have you heard a child crying, while an adult scolds or drags him out of a store? How often have you gone over to see what was wrong? How do you know that the adult is really the parent or caregiver of that child? It is frightening to think that your child might call out for help when approached by a stranger and be ignored because most adults, who could help, will not do so, for fear of embarrassing themselves or the presumed parent.

There are many excellent articles for adults and books and even coloring books out for children on this subject. They are not meant to frighten you into keeping your child at home; they are meant to make your excursions safe and worry free.

To the Mall

You CAN get your shopping done with your child along—and it can be an exciting learning experience for him. The mall or department store is a special place for anyone with its many sights, sounds, and smells. There are several things you can do with your child before, during, and after the shopping trip to make it more worthwhile for both of you.

First, here are some general tips.

■ Plan a few short trips to the store, rather than one long one. Your child's attention span is only so long and shopping is tiring even for adults.

■ Plan to go at the best time of day for your child. (Most children are at their best in the morning.) Try not to interfere with routines like naptime. Also, try not to make any other appointments or dates that day.

■ Plan ahead for several changes of pace during the trip. An active time, like window-shopping, should be followed by a relaxing time like sitting in a dressing room or having a snack.

Before shopping

▶ Look through store catalogs with your child. Choose different items in various colors and styles, cut them out, and paste them on index cards. These can be used for classifying— *"Put all the dresses in the dress store or department store." "Make piles of things to wear; things to use in the kitchen; things to play with."* Play riddle games— *"There are two of me. I keep your hands warm in the winter."*—and even department store "Concentration"— finding and matching pairs.

▶ Play store at home by having your child act out going to a store, trying things on, and buying things. Use bags and boxes from stores to wrap up what he "buys."

▶ Just before you leave or on your way, tell your child exactly what the two of you will be doing. Talk about events in order so he will have some idea what to expect and have things to look forward to. Include in your plans a ride on an escalator, if there is one, and a special snack, if possible.

While you shop

▶ Take along a sturdy pad or small clipboard and crayons. Your child can use this for drawing or making tallies of people or items. This activity is perfect for those waiting times that are unavoidable in busy stores.

▶ As you wander through each department or each small store in a mall, discuss with your child the noises, colors, odors (especially in the bakery or cosmetic departments), and textures of things. Pick up all the free samples so they can be examined at home and let your child participate in any taste or smell tests offered. Shopping excursions are terrific opportunities to help your child develop his senses and vocabulary.

▶ Ask your child's opinion on things. *"Which sweater do you like best?"* Don't forget always to ask why he prefers one thing over another. Besides making him feel very grown up and boosting his self-esteem, these questions help him develop important thinking skills.

▶ Have your child take along a few of the catalog cards as a "mini-shopping list." Let him be responsible for one purchase. Have him pick out the item, take it to the salesperson, and pay for it.

After you get home

▶ Draw a department store or mall floor plan on a large piece of paper and have your child put his catalog index cards in the places where he saw them during his trip.

▶ Recycle your trip into a collage. Have your child use parts of boxes, labels, bags, tissue paper, tags, string, or ribbon to create a permanent record of his trip. Make one for each store you visit or shopping trip you make.

To the Supermarket

If your life is anything like mine, this is the place you go most frequently (or, at least, most regularly) with your child. Luckily, some of the best lessons in math, language development, science, and social studies your preschooler can learn are hidden among the boxes, bags, and cans; on the shelves; and in the glass cases. And, if you can keep your child involved in this wonderful learning experience, he will be much less likely to get into trouble, whine, and generally disrupt your food shopping.

Involve your child when you make your shopping list. Point out the containers on your shelves of things you are almost out of and want to get at the store. Talk about meals you are planning— *"We'll have chicken tomorrow night for dinner"* and ingredients you need to make special recipes— *"We'll need flour, butter, sugar, and walnuts to make cookies this week."* Always, give him one or two special things to look out for in the store. You can make a picture shopping list for him to use by cutting actual labels off of cans, boxes, or bags of items you buy regularly and pasting them on cardboard. Make three lists with a few items on each and use a different one each week.

Here are some ideas for things to see, do, and discuss at the supermarket.

▶ In the produce department, look for unusual fruits and vegetables. Challenge your child to count all the red (yellow, orange, green, purple) vegetables and fruits he sees. Try a different color each trip. Point out the vegetables that grow underground (carrots, potatoes, beets, radishes). Compare them to vegetables that grow above ground (broccoli, lettuce, corn, peas).

▶ Look for scales in the produce department. Weigh something. Have your child guess which of two things weighs more.

▶ Look for live fish and lobsters in tanks. *"Why do they keep them in water?"*

▶ Look at the freezers. *"Why do they have doors?" "Why do you keep things in a freezer?"*

▶ Look for a bakery. *"Can you tell if the store has one without seeing it?" "Can you tell what is in the oven—cookies, bread, pies?"*

▶ Look for machines that make juice, grind coffee, or slice meat. Talk about how they work.

▶ Show your child different forms of the same food. Show him corn on the cob, corn in cans, frozen corn, cornmeal in a sack, corn muffins in the bakery, even corn chips in bags. The supermarket is the perfect place to discuss where foods come from. Point out the trucks outside the store that bring produce or boxes and cans from plants.

▶ Remember language arts by pointing out a few familiar signs, like "On Sale" or "Special This Week." Many cans and boxes are illustrated with food items that will help your child to "read" the labels.

▶ Checkout counters can be fascinating places, especially if your market has talking computers. While you are waiting in line, challenge your child to name all the items in your cart. Have him count the cans, boxes, and bags.

To the Library

You and your child have been reading together for a long time. You have probably been reading to him since he was an infant; and, perhaps recently, you've heard him "reading" to his stuffed animals.

This is a good time to make your first trip to the library together (if you haven't been already). The library is a place I go with my daughter at least once a week. There's no place to help your child fall in love with books like the library.

Most libraries today have a Children's Room or special section with small chairs and tables and often oversized pillows and even toys and puzzles to make it more inviting to young browsers. Some libraries have record players and earphones that children may use to listen to stories. Sometimes, there are also individual filmstrip projectors that children may use. Check to see if your library offers a weekly story hour for children the age of your child.

Here are some ideas to make your trip to the library together comfortable for you and educational for your child.

▶ Talk with your child about the concept of "quiet" before you go. Remind him how nice and quiet it is when you read to him at bedtime and if the phone rings or someone disturbs you, the story and the peaceful atmosphere are interrupted. Point out the people who are reading in the library and that it is important not to disturb their peace and quiet. Discuss "whispering" with your child. Play whispering games for a few days before you go. On the way to the library, practice whispering one last time.

▶ Ask the librarian to show your child around—the shelves of books that might interest him, the water fountain, the lavatory, the little tables and chairs where he can look at his selections. Your child may just want to take a few books off of the shelves and put them on a table.

▶ Talk about taking care of the books, so the next person can enjoy them, too. *"Make sure your hands are clean before you handle a book. NEVER, never scribble or underline in a book, especially if it is borrowed from the library. Use bookmarks to save your place; don't dog-ear the page."* Be sure to praise him when he does a good job of taking care of a book, not just borrowed books, but also the ones he owns. Teach your child to respect books at an early age and the lesson will last a lifetime.

▶ At the end of his first visit, let your child take out at least one book. You might want to read part of a book to your child at the library and ask *"Would this be a good book for us to take home to read?"* Don't try to match your child's interests to books all the time. Your child is an explorer; he is interested in everything for a little while. If you push any one subject at him, it can smother his interest. Let him be completely free to choose what he likes at the library. He doesn't have that many choices in his life; it will be a very satisfying experience for him just to be able to choose. This good feeling will become associated with books and the library; you couldn't ask for more.

To the Doctor

Regular visits to the doctor are facts of life for young children. When they are infants, they may not mind the poking and probing so much and they will not remember the sting of a needle from one visit to the next. But, as soon as they become toddlers, fears set in and going to the doctor can become a confusing, and often scary, experience for your child.

How can you make these necessary visits less frightening? If you can provide a setting for him to work through his fears and confusion before he goes, the doctor's office will not seem like such a strange and forbidding place. By doing some role-playing with him before a visit, you can answer some of his questions and calm his fears.

Put together some props for role-playing: tongue depressors, box of Band–Aids, fever scan tape (available at drugstores) to take his temperature, old white shirt to be used as a lab coat, alphabet eye chart (you can make one), small toy hammer for testing reflexes, and toy funnel stethoscope.

To make the TOY STETHOSCOPE, *you'll need:* two small plastic funnels and 18 inches of clear, plastic tubing. Just attach the tubing over the ends of the funnels and your child can listen to his heartbeat. He can also listen to knees bending, stomachs gurgling, and other body noises. There are several places on the body where he can pick up a heart beat; have him experiment.

First, you be the doctor and use a doll or stuffed animal as a patient. Then, invite your child to be the patient or the doctor. Finally, reverse roles. Encourage him to ask questions as you play. If you don't know the answers, you can say *"That's a terrific question. Let's remember to ask Dr. Costa when we go to see him."* Ask some of your own, when he is the doctor.

You can help your child become interested in the props by reading some stories about visits to the doctor. Try The Berenstain Bears Go to the Doctor by Stan and Jan Berenstain, Doctor Shawn by Petronella Breinburg, My Doctor by Harlow Rockwell, Mickey Goes to the Doctor by Richard Scarry, and Betsey and the Doctor by Gunilla Wolde.

Places you wait

Problems can arise before you ever see the doctor or dentist on a visit. Whether it's in the doctor's office, the beauty parlor, a restaurant, a cashier's line, or a ticket line at the movies, you have a lot of waiting to do; this is probably very difficult for your child.

There's a good reason why quiet activities for young children without a lot of movement last only a short time. Because the nerves and circulation systems in their bodies have not completely developed, it is impossible for most young children to be still for more than 10 to at the most 20 minutes at a time.

You can take care of these situations by providing your child with exercises to do which stimulate breathing and circulation without large muscle involvement that can be done in small spaces. Professor Dr. Billie Joan Thomas recommends exercises for the different areas of physical development.

Small space exercises that help your child develop STRENGTH include having him: pull against your hand; pull against his own hands; pull against your legs or knees; squat and pull up against a chair; push against your hands, fingers, or knees; push against the wall with finger, thumb, or palms of hands.

Exercises that help BALANCE develop are having your child: stand on one foot as long as possible; hold objects—keys, cup, or pencil—in one hand until they drop; walk around the edge of a rug, sofa, or room.

FLEXIBILITY is encouraged by having your child: roll his head around the neck, slowly at first, then faster, then, changing directions; bend from the waist forward, to the right, to the left, or backwards; wave forefingers in little circles, squares, or triangles; wave elbows—then hands, shoulders, feet—in small circles; reach for the ceiling; reach for his feet.

Body muscle ENDURANCE can be stimulated by having your child: grasp your finger until he must let go; stare at you until he blinks; stand in one spot until he loses his balance; say "ahhh" in a whisper until he must stop; take a breath as long as possible until he must stop breathing in—then, reverse it and breathe out for as long as possible; smile as long as possible; twirl in a circle once or twice, then, reverse direction and try it again.

PROJECTION of arms and legs is difficult in a small space, but try some of these games. Kids love them! Bring a Nerf ball (great for many emergencies) and toss it back and forth while sitting side by side. Play Toss the Empty Gum Wrapper into the Empty Coffee Cup, an Open Purse, or a Pocket.

COORDINATION exercises work well in small spaces. Have your child: play "Patty Cake" and "This Little Piggy"; put hands on body parts as you name them; flex index fingers first slowly, then faster and faster; race fingers from hips to knees and back again faster and faster.

Put your child's favorite exercises together into a five-or ten-minute routine to use anywhere. Put together some hand and finger exercises to do while your child is perched in the shopping cart. Do exercises in a chair in a crowded waiting room. All of these exercises are good for you, too. So, join in when you're bored, or take turns. These exercises will help your child's physical development and also help the waiting time pass more pleasantly.

To the Bank

Children become aware of money at a very early age. They quickly learn that it has the power to get things in stores. They know it is fun to carry around and to play with. It is difficult, however, for children to learn the meaning and value of money, when they see so many different kinds—cash, checks, credit cards, coupons—all of which can be used to pay for things. To a child, all of these seem magical and it appears very easy to buy anything he wants.

Since money is not unlimited, children can begin to learn this when they are preschoolers. Taking your child to the bank with you is the first step to discussing the meaning of money. Talk about how you put money in the bank to save it and take it out to buy things.

Make a COFFEE CAN BANK for a toddler to use to learn about coins.
You'll need: a one-pound coffee can, paper scraps, a craft knife (for adult use only), and glue. Cut slots into the lid, one for each coin size (penny, nickel, dime, quarter, half dollar). Your child can tape paper scraps around the sides of the can, collage fashion. Then, he can use the can to play games with the change in your pocket or purse. See if he can find the correct slot for each coin. This will help him sort the change by size. Of course, he can use the bank to save his own money, also.

The best way for your child to learn about money is through experience. Your child can begin getting an allowance as young as three years old. Even three pennies a week can make your child feel grown-up and be the basis for learning about saving and spending.

When there's enough money to buy something, make a special trip to the store and let your child make his selection and pay for it without your help. In this way, he can experience his savings being exchanged for something he wants. He is also getting another opportunity to make a choice. In the early years, an allowance should be used for things your child wants, but doesn't need. Later on, he can start using his savings for things he or the family needs.

TOGETHER

Make the Bleach Bottle Piggy Bank and have your child save his allowance in it.

You can talk to your child in very simple terms about the things you need to spend money on (rent, food, clothing, electricity, and transportation) and the things you choose to spend money on. Your child probably "overhears" a lot of conversation about money without your even being aware of it. He needs to hear and understand that everyone has to make choices about how they spend and save.

If your child is sharing in the family income, he should share in the family chores. Most young children love helping their parents and are able to do many jobs around the house. Never tie the allowance to how well your child does his job. If he's not doing it well or at all, find out why and remind him that he's a needed family worker. If the chosen job is too much for him, have him choose another. You might want to choose one that he can do with you.

BLEACH BOTTLE BANK

YOU'LL NEED:

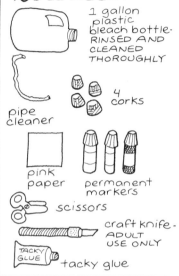

1 gallon plastic bleach bottle- RINSED AND CLEANED THOROUGHLY

4 corks

pipe cleaner

pink paper

permanent markers

scissors

craft knife- ADULT USE ONLY

TACKY GLUE — tacky glue

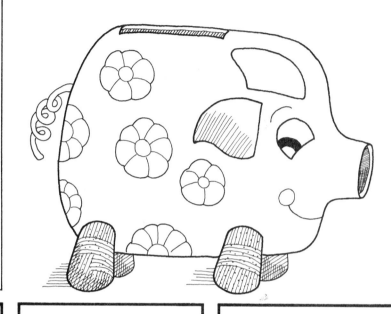

WHAT TO DO:

1. Draw a pig's face on an empty, thoroughly cleaned bleach bottle.

2. Decorate body with designs.

3. Cut out ears from pink paper and glue to bottle.

4. Cut 2" x 1/4" wide slot in top with a craft knife.

5. Glue on cork legs.

6. Poke a hole in bottle and glue on pipe cleaner tail.

To the Office

The best way to start teaching your child about the world of careers—an important topic in preschool and Kindergarten—is by sharing your own, according to psychologist, Janet Horowitz. Until my daughter visited me at my place of business, "work" and "office" were words that meant "Mommy is going away; she can't play with me now." She really needed to see and experience what I did firsthand.

With proper preparation and supervision during the visit, your child can visit your place of work with a minimum of interference to your coworkers. It also can be a worthwhile experience with lasting benefits to both of you.

Before the visit

▶ Get permission from your supervisor or your immediate superior because the more comfortable and relaxed you are, the more enjoyable your child's visit will be. Explain how important this visit is so that your child will understand what you do. State exactly how long the visit will last. Keep it short—no more than one hour. Even 15 to 20 minutes can mean a lot to an inquisitive preschooler.

▶ Choose a relatively easy day with no deadlines or meetings. You may want to go when you have a day off to minimize the pressure on you. If there are several coworkers with young children and yours is the type of business that will be totally disrupted by the appearance of a young child, you may wish to get together and organize a special day at work on a weekend or holiday. Check insurance regulations, also.

▶ Put together a bag of activities to keep your child busy, if you must concentrate on something else part of the time.

During the visit

▶ Share the things you do and let your child try them out—whenever possible. He can "read" one of your books; or, while you read, he can look at one of his own books. He can sit on your lap while you do some typing. Explain each thing as simply as possible. Your child is more likely to remember that Mommy works at a typewriter than that Mommy edits articles for a magazine.

▶ Discuss the results of your work. *"This is the magazine I work on."* Talk about your favorite things at work. *"I love writing."* Mention the things you don't like to do. *"I don't like having to make copies of everything I do."* This will help your child begin to understand the satisfactions and disappointments that everyone experiences in the working world—and, also, at school.

▶ Introduce the other people working: secretaries, telephone operators, computer operators, or people in the mailroom. See if your child can guess what they do before you tell him.

Here are some activities your child can do with general office supplies. He can make:

■ PAPER CLIP NECKLACES Show your child how to attach one clip to the other and make a necklace long enough to slip over his head.

■ LABEL PICTURES Your child can draw on and color blank sticky labels to paste onto a sheet of paper. Overlapping is fun.

■ OFFICE AUTOGRAPHS If your place of business is relatively relaxed, your child can get autographs from all the people he meets in your office.

■ TYPEWRITER PICTURES Have your child make a design with just Xs or all the letters.

■ RUBBER STAMP PICTURES Show your child how to use stamps and a stamp pad to create an "office picture."

After the visit

▶ Bind the pictures and autograph pages together into an Office Book. Your child may wish to dictate a story about his trip to your office and, then, illustrate it or "scribble write" himself.

▶ Your child will have gotten many new ideas for imaginative play. He won't just want to take your briefcase and say "I'm going to work now" anymore; he'll want to act out what you do when you get to work. Encourage this by setting up a mini-office or work place in a small area of your kitchen or playroom. On a table or shelf, have available some supplies he saw at your place of business. A toy typewriter or a few boxes set up like a computer will add to the fun. Don't be surprised if you hear him sounding just like you. Kids have a remarkable ability to mimic and it's all part of "trying on your job" to see how it fits.

▶ Read books about jobs and careers. Try What People Do All Day by Richard Scarry; Mommies at Work by Eve Merriam; and the I Want to Be books by Carla Greene.

The Important Visitor by Helen Oxenbury is about a parent who works at home. If you work at home, try to do it in a special area that your child knows is your "place of work." Make sure he understands that when you have to work in your special place, it's just like going to the office and sometimes you need to be left alone.

If you are a homemaker, share this job with your child, just like any other one. Talk about how necessary it is. Of course, let him help you, whenever possible. As you share and he helps you with household jobs, he is learning how and why all kinds of jobs are useful and important.

Remember that just as it is important for you to visit your child in his classroom or playgroup, he needs to see and learn about what you do and where you work.

toy telephone
toy typewriter
box "computer"

GETTING THERE   7

Which way?

Take a walk

    On a sunny day

    On a rainy day

Take a ride

Travel activity kit

Which Way?

As busy people, we all have many places to go every day, and getting there can be half the fun with your child. Whether you walk or ride—to the corner drugstore, across town to the doctor's office, across the state to Grandma's house—getting there can be full of rich learning experiences for your child. And, as always, a child who is interested and involved is a child who is not whining and getting into trouble.

Your child is developing directional skills whenever he goes out. The skills he will need to find his way in the woods on a 30-mile trek or to read maps of the moon as an astronaut begin in the earliest years on a trek to the supermarket.

According to Early Childhood expert, Martha Hayes, the concepts involved should be introduced in steps. You should provide enough practice in each step so that your child is completely comfortable before moving on to the next one. In addition, each step should be repeated when your child is faced with new surroundings.

1. Introduce the landmarks being passed during a walk or a car, bus, or train ride. *"There's the drugstore. Look at the park."*
2. Discuss destinations and the reasons for the trip. *"We are going to the drugstore to get some medicine for Daddy."*
3. Discuss routes to destinations as you go along. *"As we go to the drugstore, we need to turn at the park."* Don't rush things by introducing directional words, such as "left" and "right", yet.
4. On a later trip, have your child point out the landmarks and tell you where to turn. He will probably point in the direction he wants you to go.
5. Introduce your child to the directional words "left" and "right" when he is familiar with the route, and only after he is comfortable with left and right as they relate to his own body. *"We're going to turn right at the bank."* Make a point of complimenting him whenever he uses directional words in his conversation.
6. Introduce time and distance concepts. *"The farm is 75 miles away. If we leave after breakfast, we will be there in time for lunch."*

Introduce geographic directional words, such as "north," "south," "east," and "west." *"These are words that tell us where things are and what direction we might want to go. When you see the sun in the morning, it is coming up in the east. When your right hand points east, you are facing north. Your left hand is pointing west; and your back is to the south."* These concepts are very complicated and your child probably will not understand them for many years; but, if he hears the words in your conversations, he may want a simple explanation of what they mean.

For the older preschooler, you may want to make a simple map of your neighborhood with landmarks filled in. Then, together, you can mark the route of your trips in heavy crayon.

Take a Walk

On a sunny day

If you live in the city or a small town, you may often get where you're going on foot. Even if you live in a very rural area, walking with your child can do more than help his physical development.

In the words of Dr. Billie Joan Thomas, "*Approach the walk as though you are going on an adventure*" together. Even if you're on the way to the corner drugstore, it really can be a great outing for your child, one in which he can practice skills and concepts, as well as have fun. Here are Dr. Thomas' suggestions for making a walk pleasant and educational.

Adults and children obviously walk at different speeds and paces. Surprisingly, although we have more coordination and longer legs, children often walk faster than we do, when they're having a good time. If your child is very young, hold his hand and try to vary the pace from slow to fast.

If your child is older, and not likely to run out into the traffic, let him walk at his own pace. You can make a game of this. Choose an object about 20 feet away—a tree or a mailbox—and challenge your child to be a frog or a rabbit and hop to the object. Ask him how many hops he thinks he will take to get there. "*How may times can you hop there and back before I get there?*" You can have him skip, run, and walk like various animals—an elephant, duck, or bird.

Exploring your neighborhood on a walk can develop language skills, as well. Look at the environment as you go and ask your child to name, describe, compare, and classify into groups the things he sees. Ask questions like these.
■ "*What do we call the red building over there?*"
■ "*What are we standing on?*" "*What do we call the place where the sidewalk ends?*"
■ "*What color are the flowers on that lawn?*"
■ "*Which fence is longer?*" "*Taller?*"

Walking trips also give your child the opportunity to practice counting and other number skills. Together, you can count and point out sets or pairs. Try these kinds of questions.
■ "*How many cars are parked on this street?*"
■ "*How many windows can you see on that house?*"
■ "*How many cracks are there on this sidewalk?*" "*How many puddles?*"
■ "*Quick! Without counting. How many flowers are on this lawn?*" (a lot, a few) "*How many ants can you see in the sidewalk crack?*"
■ "*I see a blue mailbox. Can you find another one?*"

Choose an object and have your child guess how many you will see on your walk. It could be an object like a mailbox or fire hydrant or something more chancy like dogs, birds, or people with hats. Have your child keep a tally to see if the estimate was correct.

TOGETHER

Make an Accordion Book. Write the date and particulars—1/6/85 to the drug-store—of your walk on a page and glue the small treasures inside. Add to the book in different seasons and locations.

You also can plan shape or color walks. Informally, have your child point triangles or red things out to you or give him a small tablet with a few colors or shapes drawn. Challenge him to make a mark each time he sees something that shape or color. Take a color walk each season and compare the results.

There are many opportunities for your child to use his senses and practice his motor skills while walking. Let him explore what his body can do. Using his ears, eyes, fingers, and nose can lead to exciting new discoveries about himself and the world around him—learning he will remember a lifetime. Encourage him to:

■ see how far he can walk backwards.

■ jump as fast as he can—on one foot, the left foot, the right one.

■ close one eye and look at a house or a tree. *"Does it look the same?"*

■ listen to the sounds of the neighborhood. *"What can you hear?"* *"Name (count) the sounds."*

■ lick his finger and hold it up. *"How does the wind feel?"* *"Which direction is the wind coming from?"*

Exploring the neighborhood as you walk can develop your child's imagination and social awareness. Point out and ask him questions about occupations and similarities and differences in community helpers you see.

Stretch his imagination with questions like these.

■ *"What kind of animal might live in this hole?"*

■ *"How many people do you think live in this house?"* *"Are they young or old?"*

■ *"What kind of things are sold in this store?"*

■ *"If you could buy one thing in this window, what would it be?"* *"Why?"*

For variety, you might try a bracelet walk with your child. Place a "bracelet" of masking tape, at least an inch and a half wide, sticky side up, on your child's wrist before you leave on a walk. Tell him to pick up and place on his bracelet whatever he sees that he would like to put in his Walk Book. He may find a feather, leaf, flower, or pebble. Your child will notice things he has never seen before on his walk; little treasures can be found everywhere.

Take "scientific" walks with your child. He will love pretending to be a scientist and doing "experiments."

▶ On a windy day, give him a balloon on a string before you set out. Have him observe how the wind moves it around in the air. Help him observe the direction of the wind. *"Does it change?"*

▶ Give him a toilet paper or paper towel tube to make close observations. (The tube helps him isolate the objects he is examining.) Encourage him to examine bark, soil, or a crack in the sidewalk.

ACCORDION BOOK

YOU'LL NEED:

 scissors

glue

ruler

pencil

crayons

WHAT TO DO:

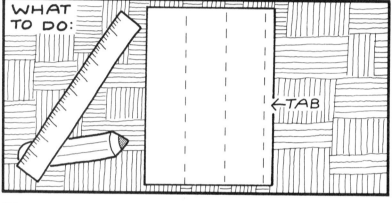

←TAB

1. Using a ruler, divide a long piece of paper into 3 equal parts. Leave ¼" extra at 1 end as a tab for gluing.

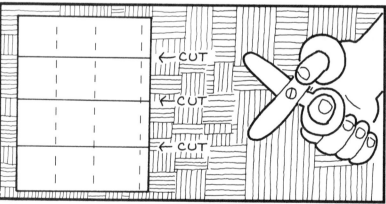

← CUT

← CUT

← CUT

2. Divide page lengthwise into 4 parts and cut across these 4 strips.

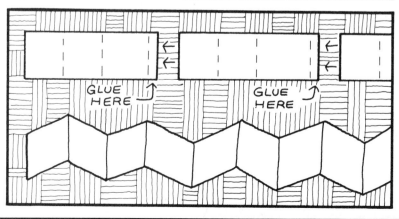

GLUE HERE

GLUE HERE

3. Attach strips together by placing glue on tabs. Accordion-fold the book.

Your child can add illustrations and you can add labels.

▶ Walk at different paces and have your child examine how he feels. Have him walk fast for five minutes and then stop. Ask *"How is your breathing?"* *"Can you feel your heart beating?"* Have him walk slowly for five minutes and observe his own reactions.

Young children love to collect things. Depending on the season and the route, encourage your child to collect twigs, leaves, seeds, wild flowers, rocks and pebbles, or feathers. Sometimes, suggest that he wear his Explorer's Knapsack on a walk. When you return home, you can play lots of learning games with his collections.

Have him put his findings in groups, classifying by color—light or dark—size, weight, or texture—smooth or rough. You might challenge him to create two piles—living and nonliving things. Older children can classify by degree—big, bigger, biggest.

He may wish to preserve some of his collections. Have him press flowers between the pages of a heavy book. Help him iron leaves between two sheets of wax paper.

He may wish to collect rubbings of various textures he encounters on a walk—tree bark, stone walls, and picket fences. These can be added to his Walk Book.

If you have a light, portable tape recorder, your child may wish to collect sounds on various walks. Compare the sounds collected on a walk through the park with those heard on a walk on a crowded shopping street.

Take a litter walk with your child. Let him carry a paper bag and instruct him to pick up papers and other "not too dirty" litter. Talk about how families are responsible for their neighborhood as well as their home.

On a rainy day
If it's a rainy day and you have to walk someplace with your child, it will be a treat for your senses. Here are some experiences to share.

▶ Smell the air. Talk about the moist, musty smell.
▶ Taste the rain.
▶ Watch puddles form. Discuss why puddles form in certain places and not in others.
▶ Observe the water running down the gutters at the side of the road. *"Where does it go?"* Place a twig in the stream and watch it move. *"Will a rock move also?"* *"Why or why not?"*
▶ Observe how much rain has fallen. Before you leave home, make a rain gauge with a ruler in a wide can. Make a note of the time you leave and when you return. Look at it when you get back.

EXPLORER'S KNAPSACK

YOU'LL NEED:

 2 large brown paper bags - 1 inside the other

2 cardboard circles (as big as half dollars)

 10' or so of string

 scissors

pencil

tape

 stapler

2 strips of cloth (2" wide x 4" long)

WHAT TO DO:

1. Draw a line down back edge, along side, front, and other side and back edge. Cut along line.

cut

The bag will look like this →

2. Fold over top of bag toward front.

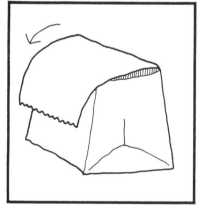

3. Staple cardboard circle to top, front and to lower front. Tie string around top circle, making knot with rest of string free.

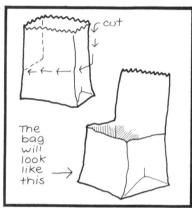

Front

4. Make slits for straps. Reinforce with tape. (Place tape over slit and re-slit).

5. Put straps through slits and tie. The length can be adjusted.

Back

EXPLORER'S KNAPSACK

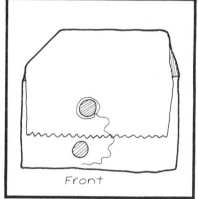

Take a Ride

There are many learning games you can play in the car or on the bus to make the time pass. These are especially useful in a traffic jam. Games make everyone feel less nervous in a tense situation, as waiting often is, and they encourage language and thinking skills, as well as developing concepts.

▶ Play "I'm Thinking of. . .," focusing on something in the car or bus. Only *yes* or *no* questions can be asked.

▶ Have a letter or number hunt. Look for either one or the other on signs, billboards, license plates, and storefronts.

▶ Have your child look out the window and try to find objects with names that begin with a special letter, such as cars, cows, curtains, canopy, and cat.

▶ Look for all things of a certain color.

▶ Tell stories; but stop just at a dramatic part and have your child add to it; then, you add another part, until finally you both think of an ending. Suggest that your child look at what's happening out the window for inspiration.

▶ Give your child a series of directions, like: wave goodbye with your right hand; touch your nose to your knee; put your finger in your ear. Speed this up, and also, slow it down. Take turns, if you are not driving.

▶ Sing songs. You may know a hundred songs; but somehow, when you're in the car, you often have a hard time remembering them. Musicologist Mary Ann Hall suggests that you make a list on an index card. You may wish to cover it with clear plastic and keep it in the glove compartment, your bag, or your pocket for emergencies. Here's her list. (Make up your own verses. Most of the old favorites can go on and on.)

OLD FAVORITES

■ "The Farmer in the Dell" Sing about all the people you're traveling with. *"Daniel's in the dell. . ."*

■ "Old MacDonald Had a Farm" Sing about a nut farm, a fruit farm, a bird farm. . .

■ "Kum Bah Yah" Sing about praying, clapping, stamping, crying.

■ "London Bridge" Sing about building it up with silly things, like ice cream cones, chicken bones, and red crayons.

■ "Flies in the Buttermilk" Sing about other circumstances, like, *"Flies in the spaghetti, shoo fly shoo. . ."* *"Goats in the closet, shoo goat shoo. . ."*

EXERCISE SONGS

■ "Eensey Weensey Spider"

■ "Where Is Thumbkin?"

■ "Head and Shoulders"

■ "The Mulberry Bush"

■ "If You're Happy and You Know It" Clap your hands, stamp your feet, tap your toe, nod your head.

TOGETHER

Prepare a few sheets of aluminum foil for your child to use in making Aluminum Foil Sculptures. Once he has created a figure, you can ask him to bend the arms, legs, and torso. Have him name his figures and tell stories about them, too. (He is developing fine motor skills along with creativity and the ability to follow directions.)

ALUMINUM FOIL SCULPTURE

YOU'LL NEED:

 scissors

large square of aluminum foil

WHAT TO DO:

1. Cut out a large square of aluminum foil (as shown below).

2. Have your child crumble up foil and mold it into a person.

3. Bend to make the foil person stand up. Try making a variety of action poses.

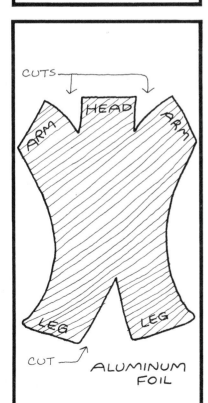

CUTS

ARM HEAD ARM

LEG LEG

CUT ALUMINUM FOIL

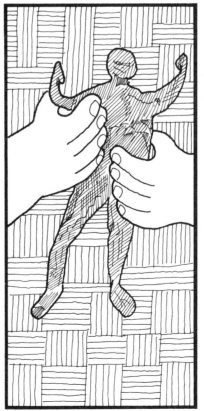

MATH SONGS

■ "One, Two, Tie My Shoe"

■ "Hickory Dickory Dock"

(*"The clock struck two.* (clap,clap)

The mouse said, "Boo."

The clock struck three.

The mouse said, "Whee."

The clock struck four.

The mouse said, "No more.")

Go all the way to ten and back again.

■ "Twenty Bottles of Pop on the Wall" (Adjust for your child's counting skills.)

Don't forget your child's favorite nursery rhymes, or teach him a new one.

▶ Bring along a tape recorder. Beforehand, record your child's favorite stories and music. Record ten different sounds and challenge your child to guess what they are. You can tape-record some riddles and mystery questions, such as *"Who couldn't be put back together again by all the king's horses and all the king's men when he fell off a wall?"*

▶ Make FINGER PUPPETS on your child's hands before you leave home. Draw a face on each of your child's fingers. Encourage him to make up a name and personality for each of the puppets, and then, tell you a story using the puppets.

▶ If there are two children in the car or on the bus, take along your **Toy Stethoscope** (directions on page 112) and use it as an intercom. Children should lower their voices when they use it.

▶ Children often get hungry on car or bus trips. Before you leave, prepare easy-to-eat snacks in plastic locking bags to take along. You might make a portable fruit salad with melon balls, pineapple chunks, seedless grapes, and strawberries for a healthy change.

▶ If you spend a lot of time in the car or on public transportation, keep the following inexpensive take-alongs on hand, stored in a paper bag or knapsack—flashlight, paperback books, small dolls, pad of paper, crayons, magic slate, magnetic puzzles, and games.

TOGETHER

Prepare Snacks on a String to take along with you.

SNACKS ON A STRING

YOU'LL NEED:

 raisins

 cheerios

dried apricots, dried apples, or prunes

large blunt tapestry needle

 popcorn

pretzels

button thread

WHAT TO DO:

1. Set out some or all of the above ingredients in individual bowls.

2. Pick favorite ingredients and set out in a pattern. Use a large, blunt needle and knotted thread to string the foods.

3. Use scissors and cut off needle. Knot ends of string and wear as a necklace. Nibble as needed.

RAISINS

DRIED APPLES

PRETZELS

CHEERIOS

POPCORN

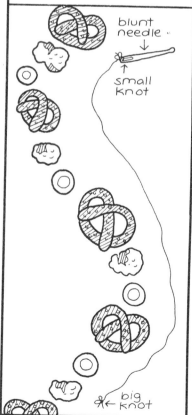

blunt needle

small knot

big knot

Travel Activity Kit

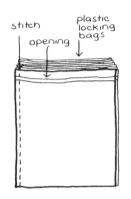

stitch
plastic locking bags
opening

For short trips or long ones, you can make your child a travel activity kit that will provide him with hours of fun. The ten activities, created by Kathy Faggella and Janet Horowitz, are stored in an easy-to-make book.

To make the book, *you'll need:* ten large (ten and one-half by eleven and one-half inches) plastic locking bags. Place them all together so that the lock opening on each one is at the top. Using heavy or doubled thread, sew along the left side with a short running stitch, about ½ inch from the edge.

Each bag is now a page. You can fill the pages with the activities described below, or invent your own.

STAMP PAD
You'll need: stamp pad with washable ink, four or five sheets of paper, black pen. Let your child make fingerprints, using the stamp pad. Have him add faces and other details with the pen.

THROUGH THE LOOKING GLASS
You'll need: magnifying glass, newspaper, comic book page. Have your child look at the paper and print through the glass.

PLAYING WITH COLORS
· *You'll need:* paint chart samples—two of the exact same color in red, orange, yellow, green, pink, purple, blue. Have your child match the same colors or make a rainbow.

FELTBOARD FUN
You'll need: homemade feltboard, 24 short pieces of yarn in various colors. Make the feltboard by gluing an eight—by—eight—inch piece of felt to a piece of cardboard of the same size. Cut yarn in three-, five-, and eight-inch pieces.

Your child can use the yarn to make pictures, designs, and patterns.

WHAT'S OUT THE WINDOW?
You'll need: paper, crayons. Before the trip, draw about eight pictures of things you might see on your way. You may want to cut them out of magazines if you don't trust your drawing skills.

Have your child circle things on the picture list that he sees out the window.

MAGNET MAGIC
You'll need: small magnet, coin, paper clip, bobby pin, tiny metal car, aluminum foil ball. Have your child try out the magnet and see what sticks to it. You might let him try various objects in your purse, also.

SEWING CARDS

You'll need: old greeting cards or cardboard with simple line drawings, hole punch, 12-inch pieces of yarn. Make holes around the edge of a greeting card or simple line drawing, glued onto cardboard. Tape one end of pieces of yarn as a needle.

Let your child "sew" in and out of holes.

CEREAL ACROBATS

You'll need: small, flat box with clear cellophane top—like a card or notepaper box—and a small handful of lightweight cereal—like puffed rice. Place the cereal in the box before you leave home. Cover and tape the edges.

Have your child briskly rub his hand over the cover, creating static electricity. He can watch the cereal "jump" to the top and dance around.

DRESS ME DOLL

You'll need: cardboard; enough felt to cover the cardboard; fabric scraps to be cut out like clothes. Cut out a cardboard doll shape. Trace onto the felt. Glue the felt cutout onto the cardboard. Use a marker to draw facial features. Cut dresses, pants, and shirts from fabric scraps.

To dress the doll, your child needs only to place clothing on the felt and press with his hand. Talk about the different kinds of clothes we wear in different kinds of weather. Talk about what goes on first, next, last.

CARDBOARD WEAVING

You'll need: piece of cardboard, six by eight inches; string or yarn. Set up the loom before a car trip. Cut slits, one-half inch apart and three-quarter inch long on opposite ends. String the loom for weaving. Make a shuttle out of cardboard. Cut a slot in the shuttle for pulling through yarn.

In the car, your child can weave in and out from one end to the other. He can make a bookmark or blanket for a doll. He will really enjoy the process.

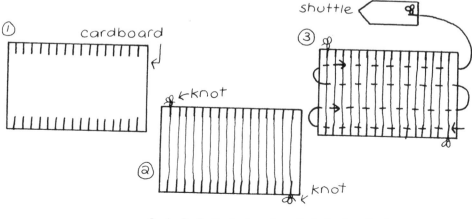

RELAXATION 8

Hobbies and games

Hobbies and Games

You work hard. You deserve time to relax and play. Not just playing with your child, but playing the games you enjoy and pursuing your own hobbies. It is very important for adults to play; it helps you relax, releases tension, and even encourages your creative thinking. It enables you to get in touch with your own interests, feelings, and skills. This, in turn, helps you tune into similar needs of your child.

But, how do you, a busy parent, play with your child and still have time for your own interests? One way is through parallel play. You can "play" beside your child, not necessarily with him. In this way, you can relax, do your own thing, and provide a model of interest and enjoyment for your child. Young children love to imitate the adults in their lives. The key is to give them similar, age-appropriate activities that make them feel grown-up, develop their own interests, and give YOU the time to enjoy your hobbies. For example, if baking relaxes you, let your child mix, roll, and form play dough at your side. If you're into painting, let him fingerpaint or use watercolors at the same time.

Now, let me go into two popular adult pastimes—woodworking and needlework—in more detail to show exactly what I mean.

Woodworking

Many times, adults overlook the terrific learning experiences young children can have working with wood because they are concerned about safety, noise, and potential problems with unfamiliar tools.

If you have a shop in your basement or garage, don't hide there from your child. With a little supervision and organization, woodworking is a safe and rewarding activity for a preschooler.

It is extremely important to teach and constantly remind your child of the proper way to use tools. Tools should only be used in your woodworking area under adult supervision. Keep storage containers and a strong magnet around for nail spills. Teach your child right away that tools should be put away immediately after each use.

POCKET:
Tuck edges
under and sew

You can create a special CARPENTER'S TOOL KIT for him. Assemble the following in an inexpensive tool box, shoe box, or small carpenter's apron—reproduce the pattern on page 47 out of heavy cloth or canvas and add pockets as shown; small, lightweight hammer—not a plastic toy; pencil; roofing nails; tape measure; glue; file; short, stubby screwdriver; screws; sandpaper; wood scraps. Eye-hand coordination is developed as your child works with wood. All tools used by your child should be regular adult tools, but small—and not too heavy. A seven oz. claw hammer and a 12 in. cross-cut hand saw are perfect for a four- or five-year-old. Keep on hand a supply of wood screws and sharp nails with large heads that are easy to handle. Also, stock up on scraps of soft wood in various shapes and sizes.

Woodworking is a wonderful way for your child to get out his aggressions and express negative feelings in a controlled atmosphere. When he's feeling frustrated or angry, put a nail in a big lump of play dough and let him at it with a small hammer. Another time, put a piece of wood in a vise and let him saw away those bad feelings.

On a more positive note, your child is practicing many basic skills by working with wood. Science ideas are developed as he learns about trees and their products. When he uses sandpaper, he learns about friction. Seeing wood become sawdust and rough boards become smooth helps him with concepts involving change. Just by observing the wood, he is learning about shapes, textures, and colors.

You can introduce woodworking to your child by having him use a light hammer to bang away at a board. In this way, he becomes comfortable handling the tool. When it is time to introduce nails, start the nail for your child. Once it no longer wobbles, he can pound it in the rest of the way himself. Soon, he will be able to start the nail by himself, using a piece of play dough or clay to hold it in place for the first few blows. A very young child can pound a golf tee into styrofoam.

Sawing is more difficult than hammering and your child will need a vise to keep the wood steady. After you show him how to use the saw a few times, he will be able to do it on his own. He will be fascinated by the process and the sawdust he creates. (Sawdust molding dough can be made by combining sawdust with wallpaper paste and water.)

Through woodworking projects, your child's creativity and imagination will develop, as he "builds" buildings, furniture, and freeform objects. Following patterns can be too much for a young child and discourage his creative urges. Let him just enjoy putting pieces together. His self-esteem will soar when he makes "something" from wood—just like you!

Needlework

Whether your hobby is sewing, needlepoint, knitting, or crocheting, your child can develop many skills and concepts through simple activities that satisfy his need to do something "just like Mom or Dad." As a toddler, he can make collages by gluing leftover bits of yarn or fabric onto cardboard. But, as soon as his eye-hand coordination allows, he can become involved in more challenging projects.

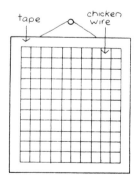

For a three- or four-year old, a structure can easily be set up to allow him to practice the basic in and out motion of weaving, which will lead someday to other needlework skills. Any structure with a uniform pattern of holes can be used. To begin, you might want to cut large holes in a piece of cardboard. Let your child use strips of fabric, yarn, even a long scarf to get a feel for the

TOGETHER

Try burlap, branch, and fruit basket weaving with your child for decorative gifts for friends and family.

in and out motion. Another easy loom can be made by stapling together the plastic rings that hold cans of soda in a six-pack. At first, your child may not follow an over/under pattern; he may interlace fabric strips at random with "unusual" results. Don't worry; it's important that he feel comfortable learning through experimentation.

As your child becomes more experienced with the concept of weaving, you can make him a box loom. Cut slits in the facing sides of a cardboard box. Stretch string across the top. Let your child weave bits of everything on this almost grown-up loom.

Through weaving, your child's eye and hand muscles work together to produce patterns. This practice in fine motor coordination, as well as experiencing direction—right to left, left to right, over and under, up and down—is developing important pre-reading skills.

Your child is developing color concepts and patterning skills, as he chooses colors and textures that repeat. He is also experiencing new words, like "thin," "thick," "smooth," and "rough."

Math skills are being developed, as your child learns or invents methods for measuring yarn and fabric. He can use the **Personal Measuring Tools**, described on page 51.

Your child will begin to look at woven structures in the environment with new interest, and, this is science. Bird's nests, beaver dams, and spider webs will hold a new fascination for him.

After he has completed a few projects on his own, your child will look at your needlework creations with new respect. He will have learned that creating things takes time. He will appreciate the skill and patience it takes to produce a dress, a handknit sweater, or a needlepoint cushion. And, most important, he will be able to share in an activity that relaxes you and gives you pleasure.

Games

Are you a game player? Do you enjoy card games, board games, backgammon, or dominoes? Your child probably cannot "play" these games yet; but he can join in the fun and you can use the game materials as teaching tools to sharpen your child's thinking skills and concepts.

With a deck of cards, your child can learn so many things. He can practice memorization and number skills through games that he plays alone or together with you. Try some of the following suggestions from Janet Horowitz with a full deck, or half a deck or less with a very young child.

WEAVING LOOMS

YOU'LL NEED:

blunt tip plastic needle

yarn-assorted colors

burlap

large branch

natural objects

thin ribbon

plastic fruit basket

hammer, nails

WHAT TO DO:

BURLAP WEAVING

Pull out a few burlap threads and replace them with yarn or thin ribbon. If necessary, a blunt tip plastic needle may be used.

Your child actually can see how fibers are woven together to make fabric by examining it, taking it apart, and putting it back together again.

BRANCH WEAVING

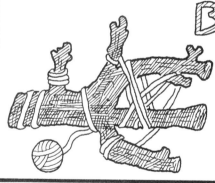

Tie or nail a large branch in private area—making sure it is below eye-level.

Knot on the yarn, 1 ball at a time, so that your child can wind it around twigs. Have on hand natural objects such as feathers, sea grass, dried flowers, to weave in also.

PLASTIC FRUIT BASKET WEAVING

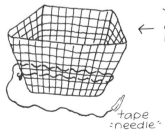

tape needle

Your child can weave yarn in and out of the holes in the basket. (These baskets make decorative containers.)

OR

He can wind yarn around basket and then weave through the yarn.

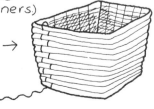

CARD GAMES TO PLAY ALONE

■ "Match the Cards"—the aces, twos, threes. . .
■ "Order the Cards"—ace, 2, 3..., ace-5..., ace-10
■ "Match by Suits"—put the clubs, diamonds, spades, and hearts into piles
■ "Order by Suits"—ace, 2, 3. . .in clubs; ace, 2, 3. . .in spades
■ "Which One Is Missing?"—remove one of the number cards in one suit and have your child find out which one is missing
■ "Concentration"—(use just the picture cards or two sets of number cards 2-10) lay the cards on a table or the floor, all mixed up; turn over two cards at a time; see if your child can find and remember a match.

CARD GAMES TO PLAY TOGETHER

■ "War to Win"—(divide a shuffled deck in half) have each person turn over a card at the same time; when there's a match of numbers, you both win
■ "More War"—turn over your cards one at a time again; but this time, the first one to get a picture card wins it
■ "Even More War"—if your child is really comfortable with his number concepts and order, try "real war" without the picture cards where the higher card wins

BACKGAMMON

If you are a backgammon player, as we are in my family, your child will be fascinated by the board, pieces, and dice. The game itself is much too complicated for a preschooler, but try these simple variations with your child for fun and learning.

▶ Stack the pieces and build towers with a toddler. Challenge your preschooler to make two towers, one of each color.
▶ Have your child copy patterns with the pieces—one red, then two white, then one red, and so on. Challenge him to add to a repeating pattern.
▶ Have your child use the round playing pieces to make other shapes. Three pieces will make a triangle; four will make a square.
▶ Have your child use the playing pieces to count. You can also use them for very simple addition and subtraction with an older child. You might want to roll a die and have your child pick the number of pieces it indicates.

BOARD GAMES

While your child cannot play Monopoly or chess, board games are important concept and skill builders for the preschool child. Games that encourage creative problem-solving—like Candyland and Chutes and Ladders—have the added advantage of developing your child's social skills, as he learns what it takes to do something in a group, waiting your turn, and cooperating. Most board games involve some form of number skills, and many provide practice in skills that will be important for reading in school. Don't hesitate to change the rules or make up your own games, using the boards and playing pieces, to suit the learning needs of your child—or just to be silly on a rainy afternoon

Reading

If, like me, one of your favorite pastimes is getting involved in a good book, you will naturally want to share your hobby with your child. You will want to instill in him a love for reading at the earliest age possible. This will give you time to enjoy your books, as he enthusiastically "reads" his.

According to reading expert, Phyllis Halloran, reading begins when the child begins to experience life itself. These experiences allow the child to react and respond to the characters, situations, and ideas in his books. Halloran maintains that *"if a child is calling out words and becoming aware of the facts in a story, he is simply calling out words and becoming aware of the facts in the story. If he is doing this plus giving thought to what is taking place, getting emotionally involved, raising questions and forming opinions, then, he is 'reading.'"*

Your child does not have to know how to read words in order to respond to a book. He can read the pictures or recall a story as it has been told to him. He must be told from the earliest age possible that he is "reading" when he discusses pictures, gives his opinion on characters, and compares situations in his books to his own experiences.

Phyllis Halloran has a number of suggestions to help you develop a positive attitude toward books and reading in your child. If you are an avid reader, they will be easy and pleasant to incorporate into your daily routine. Your reward will be a child who respects and appreciates your hobby.

▶ Read to your child every day—babies, too. The warm feelings that come from this shared time on your lap as often as possible will rub off on the reading experience.

▶ Surround your child with books of all sizes, shapes, and colors. Try to include books that appeal to many senses.

▶ Reassure your child that wordless books are for people of all ages. They have exciting stories, characters, and ideas. An added bonus is that they encourage creativity. Some suggestions: The Red Balloon by Ilea Mari; Anno's Journey by Mitsumasa Anno; The Chicken's Child by Margaret Hartelius; The Egg Book by Jack Kent; and Frog, Where Are You? by Mercer Mayer.

▶ Let your child see you reading for pleasure as often as possible. Let him also see you handling books with respect.

▶ You may very well read the newspaper, too. Let your child participate in this experience also by setting up a game for him to play with yesterday's edition or a section you've finished. First, you go through the newspaper, looking for objects in pictures, ads, and photographs that your child can easily identify. Make a picture list of about five items you have seen. Then, give the list and the newspaper to your child and have him circle the items as he finds them right in the paper.

If your child can recognize letters, give him a page—one with lots of large type, perhaps, a full page ad—and have him find all the letters in his name, put a circle around all the "Js," put a line under the "Ds," and as a real challenge, try to find all 26 letters of the alphabet.

If there are comics in your newspaper, occasionally take out your child's favorite strip, and cut apart the individual frames. See if he can put them in the correct sequential order. Try to find a wordless comic strip with only three or four frames.

▶ Take your child regularly to the library. (See page 111.)
▶ Ask your child for his opinion about a story or a character.
▶ When you read together, encourage him to ask lots of questions. Try to anticipate questions he might have and stop often, so he doesn't feel like he's interrupting you. Weave definitions of hard words right into the story.
▶ Discuss favorite books with your child without making it seem like a quiz with right and wrong answers.
▶ Point out the authors of books. *"Here's another book by Dr. Suess. I wonder if it rhymes like* Green Eggs and Ham?*"* In this way, your child will become more aware of individual books.

Besides entertainment, books are bridges for your child from one experience to another, from ideas to feelings, from problems to solutions. Books can ease your child's transition from home to school, from everyday routines to a vacation, from only child status to being a big brother or sister.

When your child reads a book about a character with a problem similar to one that he is facing, he feels less alone. He sees that others share his problem, and, more important, that there are ways to cope with it. When he discusses the book with you, he can talk about his own feelings and ideas indirectly by attributing them to the character in the story— often an animal. For example, I Won't Be Afraid by Joan Hanson explores many simple fears that young children have; Feelings by Barbara Polland helps your child express a variety of feelings through photographs of real life situations.

Recently, many children's authors have written books about major childhood problems, fears, and special events. Disease, divorce, physical handicaps, death, peer relationships, separation, adoption, the birth of a new baby, how to deal with strangers—you can find books on these sensitive issues and others on the shelves in your bookstore or children's library. Children's Books for Times of Stress by Ruth Gillis lists titles and authors under each problem. The Open Family Books by Sara Bonnett Stein have stories and information for both parents and children on such topics as death, adoption, and handicaps.

When you read one of these books, talk about the characters and the plot, but never pressure your child to identify with the characters. If he is ready to deal with the situation on a personal level, he will do so freely; but even if he isn't ready, the story and sharing time may be a great comfort.

Books can also be bridges to creative activities for you and your child. Books about colors, like Is It Red? Is It Yellow? Is It Blue? by Tana Hoban and Little Blue and Little Yellow by Leo Lionni, can stimulate lots of activities that deal with colors from naming the colors in the room to painting experiences.

One of the best ways to introduce your child to fine art and artists is through his books. When you read together, talk about the illustrations, how they were done, and what kind of materials might have been used. Compare the styles of different illustrators.

Activities where you read a book, discuss the illustration, and model a project from the content line of the book or the artist's style are called patterning books. If you and your child enjoy these, you might try making paper collage characters, like the ones in Zoophabets by Robert Tallon. This project could then inspire a trip to the zoo. Thus, a book has become the springboard to an art experience and an outing.

Bruno Munari's Zoo is another excellent book to read in connection with a trip to the zoo. Talk about the animals. Then, have your child cut pictures of animals out of magazines, like National Geographic's World and Ranger Rick, and paste them in his own book.

Creating his own books is an important part of encouraging your child's involvement with reading. These books can hold collections of favorite drawings or fingerpaintings. Any of these projects take on an added dimension when the books contain written stories, dictated by your child or "scribble written" himself, just so he can experience what writing is all about. In this case, don't worry about spelling, words, or anything. Be sure to have him "read" you what he has written when he is finished, whether he has written or dictated it. He may not remember all the words, but he will begin to see the relationship between the spoken and written word. He might even enjoy tracing over the letters you write or copying them.

As he gets older, your child may want to dictate explanations or comments on drawings he has done in his books. He will probably need some guidelines to dictate a whole story. After reading a favorite story together, you might go over the high points in the story with your child. Have him draw pictures to illustrate each major event. Then, have him put the pictures together in order and dictate his own version of the story. This is terrific practice in the skill of sequencing and also it helps him become more aware of details.

Pets, favorite toys, holidays, and vacations also provide opportunities for your child to "write" a personal book. Create all kinds of blank books that will invite your child to write in them. You can be very imaginative with the covers and even the pages.

Should you teach your child to read?

All of the suggestions thus far have related to developing a love of books and reading in your child. A by—product of many of these activities may be practice in skills and concepts necessary for learning to read, but this is not their main purpose.

As a former reading teacher, I don't usually recommend that parents "teach" their children the mechanics of reading at home. This can be very frustrating for everyone concerned. Each child learns to read in his own time and in his own way. If he is pressured, or taught too soon, or in the wrong way, it may turn him off from reading for life. Don't listen to friends who swear that their preschoolers can read the encyclopedia or relatives who remember that you started reading before you were three!

Your child, however, may be very anxious to learn the meanings of all those letter and word symbols before he starts school. If this is the case, ask yourself the big question *"Is my child ready to begin the reading process?"*

You've probably heard the term *"reading readiness"* used in reference to Kindergarten and first grade curriculums. Perhaps you'd like your child to arrive in school "ready to read." Readiness for reading means that your child is ready emotionally, physically, socially, and, of course, intellectually.

Take a look at the checklist which follows prepared by Janet Horowitz. As you observe your child's natural behavior over a period of a few weeks, ask yourself these questions to determine just how ready your child is for the technical aspect of reading readiness.

PHYSICAL READINESS
■ Are your child's eyes and ears functioning properly? If your child can't see printed letters and words clearly, he won't be able to read. If he can't hear letter sounds accurately, he won't be able to put sounds together with the correct letters they represent.
■ Can your child see small items and tell the difference between them—for example, the two sides of a coin?
■ Can he be understood by strangers when he speaks? Is his pronunciation clear?
■ Can he speak up in a group?
■ Can he string beads, cut paper, and bounce a ball?
■ Can he copy simple shapes?
■ Can he color in and stay within the lines of a simple shape?
■ Can he turn the pages of a book by himself?

TOGETHER

Little Blue and Little Yellow has perfect illustrations to discuss. Lionni has a distinctive style, which your child can use as a model for his own artwork. **Torn Paper Pictures** develops the concepts of colors and shapes, as well as the skills of tearing and pasting.

TORN PAPER PICTURES

YOU'LL NEED:

GLUE
glue

pieces of white paper

pieces of colored tissue paper

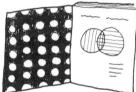

LITTLE BLUE AND LITTLE YELLOW by Leo Lionni

typewriter or pen

WHAT TO DO:

1. Read LITTLE BLUE AND LITTLE YELLOW aloud to your child.

2. Go back over story and discuss how the author used torn paper to illustrate it.

3. Tear pieces of tissue paper and glue on paper to make a picture.

4. Have your child dictate his own story about his picture.

5. Type or write the story and mount it on the picture.

INTELLECTUAL READINESS

■ Is your child interested in looking at magazines and books?
■ Is he aware of the world of print on signs, mail, and cereal boxes?
■ Is he interested in the meanings of words?
■ Has he asked to see his name in print?
■ Does he enjoy listening to stories?
■ When he has heard a story, can he recall what it is about?
■ Can he tell a simple story in the correct order—beginning, middle, end?
■ Can he guess what might happen at the end of a story?
■ Can he memorize a short poem or song? Can he rhyme?
■ Can he draw a picture and tell you about it?
■ Can he carry on a meaningful conversation?
■ Does he use a large variety of words easily?
■ Does he understand the meaning of words, such as "big," "little," "front," "back," "up," "down?"
■ Can he pay attention to a task for at least ten minutes?
■ Can he make up nonsense words?

EMOTIONAL READINESS

■ Can he accept changes in the routine without getting upset?
■ Can he see a task through to the end?
■ Does he take pride in his work?
■ Is he ready and eager for new experiences?
■ Will he do what an adult asks or does he resent it?

SOCIAL READINESS

■ Is he able to cooperate when playing with others?
■ Can he take on and carry out new responsibilities?
■ Can he follow simple directions?
■ Is he able to share things?
■ Can he wait his turn when playing and accept help from adults?
■ Can he take care of the materials he uses?
■ Can he work on his own?

The activities throughout this book help your child practice all of the skills above. If your child can do all of these things by the time he is in Kindergarten, first grade, or even second grade, he is still right on track.

Let's say, for example, that your child has already mastered all of these skills and is eager to learn more about letters and words. Now, take a look at your "readiness for teaching" your child to read. Again, there's a checklist to help your self-evaluation.

■ Have you carefully watched your child and thought about his readiness?
■ Have you corrected any speech, vocabulary, hearing, or vision problems your child might have by seeking professional help?

■ Do you think you will succeed? (This comes through to your child and can effect his progress.)

■ Are you willing to praise any progress and not use criticism or punishment if your child is not meeting your expectations?

■ Are you willing to brag about your child's progress—no matter how small—to others?

■ Do you have lots of books around for your child to choose from?

■ Do you read aloud to him on a regular basis?

■ Most important, do you transmit your own joy of reading to your child?

If you and your child are ready and eager to learn more about letters and words, there are a number of excellent alphabet books you can look at together. At this point in his career, learning the letters should be a game to your child. All of the suggestions that follow are fun and should be used in the spirit of playfulness.

■ Applebet and ABC by Clyde Watson (rhymes)

■ Animal Alphabet by Bert Kitchen

■ ABC's by Brian Wildesmith

■ ABC Book by Bruno Munari

■ The Kitten's ABC by Clare Turlay Newberry

■ Alphabet Book by Nedo Beck

■ Hey Look at the City ABC by Sandy Grant

Follow up these reading experiences with letter walks or looking for things in a room that all begin with the same sound. Have your child cut pictures from old magazines and make a Letter Name Book with the first letter written by each picture. Another possibility is to make a page for each letter and have your child look for objects that begin with each one.

The Best Word Book Ever by Richard Scarry is the best book ever to introduce your child to words that stand for objects. Even before he zeros in on the words themselves, he will love naming the familiar objects on each page. Label objects around the house with the words on index cards, similar to what is done in the book.

Playing with letters and words is one of the best concrete ways to introduce your child to reading mechanics. Just remember the name of this game should always be FUN!

Television

Like books, television is a way for many people to relax, get information, and be entertained. TV does not stimulate the imagination the way a book does; but its merits for children are sometimes overlooked because it is often overused and misused by today's families.

The issue of TV watching for young children is not just black and white. But, since TV is a fact of life in most homes today and since most children observe their parents watching TV for relaxation and entertainment, the question is not whether or not to permit your child to watch, but rather how much to let him watch and under what circumstances.

Studies show that preschool children watch on the average of 35 hours of television a week. That's five hours a day, seven days a week. That's an awful lot of time spent on one activity; an activity that, if your child just sits alone watching program after program, only has limited effects on his growth.

Young children need to develop their muscles and coordination by running, climbing, jumping, drawing, fingerpainting, modeling with dough, cutting—all of which they must practice often. Once he turns on the set and adjusts the channel, picture, and volume, your child has finished practicing his motor skills. Shows like Sesame Street and Romper Room do encourage children to participate actively at home in child-centered exercises, dancing, and movement games, but most programs do not.

Some TV programs help children with their social and emotional development by showing them lots of people in many different social situations displaying a wide variety of emotions. The TV set, however, cannot give your child a hug or show him what concepts like sympathy and understanding are all about.

TV can affect your child's language development to some extent. He can learn words and phrases from characters on TV, but language must be used for it to grow and be really understood by the young child. He needs many opportunities to repeat new words and phrases in the context of his daily life.

On the positive side, what your child watches on TV can introduce him to people, places, and situations that probably we, and certainly our parents, were unaware of as children. It can also be a springboard to exciting learning experiences. The issue is whether or not watching a particular program at a particular time will contribute to the richness of your child's life.

The issue is also why the TV set is on from your point of view. When you can't be with your child and it is important for him to be quietly busy, television is one answer. If the program is appropriate and you've given your child a choice of watching or doing something else, like reading a book or doing a puzzle, then you don't have to feel guilty about using it to give you that all important ''breathing space'' in your day.

Can TV be a teaching tool?

Yes, the television can have a positive influence on your child's development. Here are some suggestions on how to make the most of it. (Many of these ideas come from ACT, Action for Children's Television, a group of parents and professionals who care deeply about what is offered to our children on TV.)

First, select the programs your child watches carefully. Set a TV time limit—no more than two hours daily. Look at the weekly TV schedule and make a list of acceptable programs from which your child can choose. Many programs are designed to teach concepts and skills and portray real feelings and social situations. These include Sesame Street, Romper Room, and Mister Roger's Neighborhood. Others, notably cartoons, give a false picture of the world that can be dangerous for your child. He gets the wrong message when he sees a cartoon character put his finger in a light socket and walk away unharmed or walk off a cliff without getting hurt.

Look for nature specials and animated versions of children's classics, which often come on in prime time during the holidays. If your child watches a dramatization of a children's story, be sure to have the book on hand for follow-up reading. Many specials may not be specifically for preschoolers; so plan to be there yourself, or enlist another adult or older child to answer any questions your child might have.

Always sit with your child if the program he is watching might be scary. Answering questions on the spot and clearing up any wrong ideas about what is happening will prevent real fears and even nightmares from bothering your child later on. Talk about the difference between real and make-believe.

Watch shows with your child so that you can observe what he really enjoys and discuss it with him. *"Do you like comedies or shows about animals?"* Talk about why he enjoys them; this will help both of you make his weekly choices the right ones.

With an older child, you may wish to make a weekly TV viewing guide. Set aside a special time each week, maybe on Sunday afternoon, and look over YOUR list of acceptable shows together and make choices for the coming week. Use colored markers to circle the selected programs in the weekly newspaper guide. Put the chart near the TV and refer to it each day.

You should also explain to your child why you enjoy the programs you do. There's nothing wrong with your child watching with you a few carefully selected adult programs that you enjoy. But, always keep some books and games around, in case his attention wanders. *"You didn't seem too interested in the program I was watching. You played with your teddy bear. This kind of show is better for older people."*

Even if you plan to use the time your child is watching a totally appropriate show to get some work done around the house, try to plan your work in the same room as the TV set. Just glancing at the program occasionally can give you ideas for follow-up activities later in the day. *"They were skipping on* Romper Room *today; would you like to skip to the mailbox?"* Being there for the last two minutes of Sesame Street will tell you which numbers and letters have been featured in that episode so you can practice them through your own games and activities. *"You learned about the letter A on TV today. Can you find any As on this page in the newspaper?"*

Make a habit of turning the TV off when a program is finished. Have a specific game or activity planned so the transition to no TV will be easier. If your child can't go outside to play, perhaps there can be a story about Ernie to read together when Sesame Street is over. Encourage your child to talk about who was on the program and what happened after the set is off. This helps him develop recall and language.

Using a video recorder

By the year 1990, a large percentage of our homes will be equipped with VCRs or other video disc recorders and players. This revolution in TV technology is terrific for your child in many ways.

Most obviously, videotapes of excellent movies and programs for young children are widely available, and you can preview them before showing them to your child.

You can tape programs which your child might otherwise miss because they are on at an inconvenient time or after his bedtime. You can tape that wonderful afternoon children's special on adoption that happens to air on a sunny day and save it for the next rainy one. You can tape a National Geographic wildlife special that goes on at eight o'clock at night to be shown at a more appropriate time.

If you have not chosen to make a list of weekly programs for your child to watch, then he may be in the habit of "junk viewing," a real concern to child development experts. Your child may be in the habit of watching shows he doesn't particularly like, just because they're the "best thing on." He wouldn't read a book or play a game that didn't interest him, but because the TV is such a passive activity, he will sometimes watch "mindlessly."

With a video disc player, your child, looking for television entertainment, can choose from a group of carefully selected, age-appropriate materials. Like a favorite book, he can put on a favorite cassette or disc and be whisked away to Oz or down the rabbit hole to Wonderland or into the ocean on a voyage with Jacques Cousteau. He can also turn it off to be continued later, if another fun activity comes up.

Once on a cassette or disc, a program becomes like a book with many skills to be learned from it. Since they can be replayed, programs can be used to teach sequence, cause and effect, inference, and even predicting outcomes because you can stop the tape right before a climax in the story and practice this skill. Character's feelings and reasons for doing things can be more easily understood when the tape is replayed and your child can review the events that led up to decisions and emotions. In addition, during the taping process, you can do simple editing jobs, like deleting offensive material and commercials.

Controversy over commercials

If you could tape each program your child watches and edit out the commercials, you would be eliminating many of the objections voiced by the experts against TV for children. If you could always sit with your child and prove that many foods pushed by commercials cause cavities and many of the toys shown break too easily, you would save yourself a lot of arguing in the supermarket or toy store.

But, since impossible, you can begin to teach your child about commercials and develop his critical thinking skills. Commercials create false needs and "use" children to get parents to buy products. Here are some suggestions from Janet Horowitz on how you can teach your child not to believe everything he hears or sees on TV.

▶ First, develop your child's awareness of what commercials are, whenever you watch TV with your child. When a commercial appears, talk about what it is doing—trying to sell us something. Let him guess what is being sold. Develop thinking and recall skills by asking questions like: *"Do we use this product in our house?" "What do we use like it?"*

▶ Products are not always what they look like on TV. Claims made are often misleading and this needs to be pointed out to your child *"Isn't that silly? No one could possibly clean the kitchen floor that fast." "Remember that toy we saw in the shop window? It didn't look half as big as it does on TV."* Read Ralph Proves the Pudding by Winifred Rosen for a look at this problem.

▶ Use distraction techniques during commercials to take your child's mind away from the "hard sell" on the screen. Commercials stop the story, so keep it going by talking about it during the commercial. Discuss the parts you enjoyed. Ask your child what he thinks is going to happen next. Let him draw an ending on paper with crayons or markers.

▶ Turn off the sound and concentrate on the healthy aspects of the commercial. For example, cereal ads often show families eating a well-balanced breakfast. Talk about this. Have a few old magazines near the set for your child to browse through and find pictures of other breakfast foods.

▶ Whenever you see a really offensive commercial during a children's program, complain about it. ACT is working to eliminate all commercials from children's programming.

SPORTS

Pregame warm-up

Mind and muscles

Exercising for fitness

Playing the big games

Golf

Bowling

Frisbee

Tennis, squash, racquetball

Baseball

Watching the big game

Pregame Warm-Up

Your child has many skills to develop before he begins organized sports. Because most sports involve many basic skills and often combine the abilities of different players, young children are not usually introduced to them until the ages of eight or nine. It is the activities your child does now, however, that prepare him for later sports. The chart by Martha Hayes on the following page shows at the top simple activities that most young children enjoy. Along the left side are the names of many popular organized sports. The checkmarks indicate which activities are helpful in developing skills necessary for the sports. By introducing these activities to your child now, you are helping him develop the muscles and coordination necessary for later sports. Along with the workouts, he will enjoy reading about animal athletes in the Sierra Club Growing Up Books by Derek Hall and the The Animal Athlete's Board Book Series by Kenneth Lilly.

Along with developing your child's motor skills in preparation for organized sports, it is equally, if not more, important to develop your child's self-image and attitudes toward competition—winning, losing, and just "playing the game." You want your child to feel like a "winner," no matter what the score is or how successful he seems to the outside world.

Your child was probably exposed to competition in the cradle, when he heard you discuss with other parents which child slept through the night first, stood up first, and took his first sip from a cup. Later, you talked about who walked, learned his colors, and went to the potty first. As you made innocent comparisons, your interest in the development of other children put your child in direct competition with them. When you compare your child's accomplishments with others, he can begin to feel that somehow he's not okay if he's not first or best. Even a toddler can get discouraged and attitudes may form that will last a lifetime.

Here are some suggestions to help your child's physical and emotional development—to make him feel like a winner all the time.

▶ Your child's body structure will tell you the activities for which he is best suited. When you understand his capabilities, you can help him develop the skills and the positive attitude he needs to enjoy sports.

▶ Remember that your child will learn physical activities in his own way at his own pace when he is interested and ready.

▶ He will approach activities in his own way—depending largely on how he has experienced the activity when he was just a spectator.

▶ Your child probably will want to try a physical activity more if he does not feel that he must take part just to win your approval. Try not to push him to learn skills in a competitive way.

▶ Your child should be the one to decide when he should begin a more organized activity and how well he should play it. You want him to enjoy "playing the game," not just winning it. A child who is pushed to win in a competitive way becomes an adult who needs to win in order to feel good about himself.

▶ Help your child feel good about what he's doing by encouraging him and not comparing him to anyone else. Put the emphasis on how hard he is trying or the progess he has made, rather than the final accomplishment. Be aware of the hidden meaning in statements like the following: *"I'm so proud of you for winning the race,"* (*"I wouldn't be proud of you if you didn't win the race."*) and *"Congratulations! You jumped much farther than your sister did."* (*"You're supposed to compete with your sister and do better."*)

▶ When you introduce a game or activity to your child, focus on the fun of the experience, not winning or getting it right. Each time you play, notice his improvement, celebrate his progess, and downplay who wins or loses.

▶ Finally, take a look at yourself and your own attitudes. You are your child's first, and most influential, model. Do you feel good about yourself, whether you win or lose? While you may play to win, also play to enjoy and let your child share your enjoyment. You don't want your child to miss out on any of the exciting sports activities and games that are ahead for him.

	RUNNING	THROWING	JUMPING	CLIMBING	PEDALING	PUSHING/ PULLING	HITTING	KICKING	SUPPORTING ONE'S WEIGHT	BALANCING	
TENNIS	✓						✓				
ICE SKATING										✓	
SKIING	✓		✓	✓						✓	
RIDING (HORSES)				✓	✓						
GOLFING	✓						✓				
ARCHERY						✓	✓				
CROQUET							✓				
HORSESHOES		✓					✓				
GYMNASTICS	✓		✓	✓					✓	✓	
SOCCER	✓						✓	✓			
SOFTBALL	✓	✓					✓				
BASEBALL	✓	✓					✓				
BASKETBALL	✓	✓	✓				✓				
TRACK AND FIELD	✓	✓	✓		✓		✓	✓			
FOOTBALL	✓	✓	✓			✓	✓				
VOLLEYBALL		✓	✓			✓	✓				
SWIMMING			✓					✓		✓	
BICYCLING					✓					✓	
HIKING	✓			✓						✓	
JUDO							✓	✓			
WRESTLING						✓					

Mind and Muscles

Before he is able to play tennis with you or baseball on the family team or ride a horse or wrestle, your child has to develop his mind and muscles. His muscles need his mind to control them and his mind needs his muscles to carry out its plans. They have to develop together for either one to be effective. The mind and muscles must start developing as a team almost from the time your child is born. You can help this development along by encouraging your child to explore the world through activities that stress muscle control and eye-hand coordination.

Dr. Billie Joan Thomas has specific suggestions for developing strength, balance, flexibility, endurance, coordination, and relaxation through simple activities. These activities require no special apparatus or expensive toys. Some of them are discussed on pages 112–113 as activities to do in waiting rooms or when in line. Here are some more active things to do at home.

STRENGTH
■ Let very young—two-to-four-year-old—children: push a ball away as hard as possible; stomp on the rug or the ground.
■ Let older children—five-through-eight years old: play tug-of-war with a knotted rope, old rag, garden hose; lean against the house and try to push it over; try to push or pull you over; try to lift heavier and heavier objects; play with running toys—wagon, hand mower; ride tricycles or big wheels; swing.

BALANCE
■ Let very young children: stand on one foot; hop; skip; stand on small blocks; sit on the edge of a low chair.
■ Let older children: put a wooden beam on the ground and walk on it, first on the flat side, and later on the end; walk backwards and sideways; ride a bike; climb trees.

FLEXIBILITY
■ Let very young children: lie on the floor and wiggle all around; hold your hands while you dip their bodies at the waist; crawl through different-sized cardboard boxes.
■ Let older children: wave each part of their body, as you name it; move body parts sideways, back and forth, in circles and squares; move like snakes and spiders; reach forward and back, first with one hand and then the other; do simple yoga exercises.

PROJECTION
■ Let very young children: drop plastic or paper cups; roll balls into a basket; throw soft toys; reach for objects; kick balls and pebbles.
■ Let older children: play catch; throw stones in puddles; sit on the floor and kick balls with legs; lay on the floor and kick balls with head; throw horseshoes; throw rubber—tipped darts; throw pennies in a well; play croquet.

TOGETHER

Try Six Things to Do with a Beanbag.

6 THINGS TO DO WITH A BEANBAG

A beanbag is a unique toy. It can be tossed like a ball but won't bounce away. It is heavy enough to make it easy to catch and grip and it feels great to hold. Make a beanbag from felt or fabric. It can be square, round, or fancy-shaped. Fill it with dried beans, uncooked rice, or bird seed.

WHAT TO DO:

1 JUGGLING

Use 1 beanbag and toss it from left hand to right hand and back again. Toss 1 beanbag as high as possible and catch it in 2 hands and then 1 hand. Toss 2 beanbags and try to catch in each hand simultaneously. Toss 2 beanbags alternately and catch in each hand alternately.

2 TARGET TOSS

Draw 3 chalk circles on pavement or rug. Each should be 3' apart. Place a "START" line about 5' from the first circle.

TO PLAY: Stand on "START" and toss beanbag into closest circle. If successful, toss it into another one farther away. Then, see if it can be tossed into the farthest one.

3 FOOT TOSS

Have your child sit on a chair and place a beanbag on his right foot, toss it slightly and catch it back on his foot. Now, toss it to the left foot. Stand and place beanbag on right foot. Toss and catch it in hands.

4 RING THE BELL

Hang a sturdy bell by a heavy string from a tree branch. Mark a "START" line about 6' away.
Have your child toss beanbag and try to ring the bell.

5 BEANBAG SCOOP

Save 2 gallon-size plastic milk cartons with handles. Thoroughly washed empty bleach bottles work well also. Cut away bottom- as in diagram.
Have your child toss and catch a beanbag in a scoop.

FLIP FLOP ROPE 6

BEANBAG

Two adults hold both ends of a jumprope, letting the center of the rope touch the ground. Place a beanbag over the rope where it touches the ground.

TO PLAY: Have your child stand near the middle of the rope. The adults pull the rope and make the beanbag flip into the air. Your child catches it!

ENDURANCE

■ Let very young children: grasp your finger until they must let go; stare at you until they must turn away; stand until they fall.

■ Let older children: run until they have to stop; smile until they cannot; stare until they must blink; arm wrestle; jump rope as long as possible, twirl in circles until they fall; pedal a bike until they must stop.

COORDINATION

■ Let very young children: tap different body parts together; hold a cup and walk; close eyes and walk; hop sideways.

■ Let older children: hold hands to side and bring index fingers—thumbs, fingers—together as fast as possible; close eyes and walk in a line; rub head and stomach at the same time; walk with head between knees; stand on one foot and make circles in the air with the other foot; carry paper clips—cotton balls, marbles—on a large spoon; skip, hop, and jump to music; climb trees.

Exercise for fitness

If you're into exercising, your child will want to join in the workout, whether it's Jane Fonda, Jack LaLanne, or your own invention. He will really benefit from a regular, well-planned fitness program. Since your child's body—its capabilities and needs—is different from yours, you have to be careful when he joins in your activities.

Here are some DOS and DON'TS from Jean Stangl to keep in mind, as you keep fit together.

■ DO provide a safe environment. Inside, exercise on a carpeted surface or mats, and, outside, use the grass or similar soft surface.

■ DO have your child wear loose, comfortable clothing and shoes. Exercising barefoot provides added tactile awareness.

■ DO provide time for warm-up, exercise, and cool-down. This is important for everyone. Guide your child with slow stretches to prepare the body, work up to active exercises, maintain for a few minutes, and then, slowly, bring the body back to normal.

■ DO provide developmental exercises in sequence. Have your child start with simple exercises and work up to more complicated ones. Change your routine often, so your child doesn't get bored.

■ DO practice reverse deep breathing with your child. Push out the stomach as you inhale deeply; draw the stomach back toward the spine as you exhale deeply. This allows the lungs to fill more fully and exercises the chest muscles.

■ DO try to build your child's endurance. Seventy-five percent of today's young children cannot run in place for a minute. Set a timer for fifteen seconds the first day, and increase ten seconds daily.

■ DON'T let your child do Atlas-type exercises, feats of strength, or heavy pushing or pulling. These exercises enlarge, stretch, and strain his developing muscles and can cause permanent damage.

■ DON'T let him do exercises that jerk, pull, or strain his muscles or ligaments.

REVERSE
DEEP BREATHING

1. Inhale   2. Exhale

Tummy out   Tummy in

Slow, easy stretching and bending movements are best for your developing child.

■ DON'T let him do forced toe touches with stiff knees. This places too much strain on his lower back and the muscles and ligaments in the back of his legs. Instead, have him flex his knees and bend forward slowly, only as far as he is comfortable.

Flex knees   Flex knees

■ DON'T let him do very deep knee bends or duck walks. He can damage the muscles and cartilage that support the knee and this may cause later knee problems.

■ DON'T let him do leg lifts with both legs straight. This tilts the pelvis forward and places strain on his lower back. Have him bend one knee and place the sole of the foot on the floor. Then, he can slowly lift and lower the other leg.

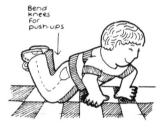

Bend knees for push-ups

■ DON'T let your child do sit-ups with stiff legs. This strains his lower back, too. Have him bend his knees with feet flat on the floor and slowly roll up and down.

■ DO be sure to praise your child for what he can do and build on his strengths. Make your child feel good about whatever he does. This should be the beginning of a lifelong fitness program.

If your exercise program includes yoga, encourage your child to join in as often as possible. The purpose of yoga for children is to help them feel good about themselves. Yoga helps children relax in order to enjoy and experience fully both movement and rest.

There are yoga exercises to release muscle tension, increase blood circulation, and improve breathing, posture, and balance. Through yoga, your child can use his imagination more creatively. His ideas will flow freely as he feels relaxed, supported, and accepted.

Invite your child to participate with you in yoga exercises and create a relaxing atmosphere through your words, tone, voice, touch, and your own body language. Start with the Lotus Position and go on to others.

Read Be a Frog, a Bird, or a Tree by Rachel Carr for specific exercises. There are one or two exercises on each page, illustrated with a black-and-white close-up of a child doing the exercise. There's an excellent chapter at the end just for parents.

You may wish to use just one or two yoga exercises at a time for limbering up or relaxing after a very active period. Between exercises or at the end of an exercise, be sure to do what is called a cleansing breath. This reenergizes the body before going on to the next activity.

If you do not practice yoga now, you might look into it as an activity you and your child can learn together. Yoga is a wonderful way to share good feelings —and feeling good!

Playing the Big Games

Your child watches you while you play your favorite sports. He doesn't want to hear that he's too young to play. He can't understand why he must develop his motor skills and coordination before he will truly be able to participate. So, until that time, here are some kid-sized versions of popular sports that your child can enjoy.

HIT THE BALL....

INTO a tin can

THROUGH a tin can

UP and INTO a tin can

AROUND 4 tin cans

Golf

Use old tennis balls, a cardboard tube from a long roll of wrapping paper, and tin cans large enough to fit a tennis ball. Set up a small course on a carpeted surface. Have your child hit the tennis ball with the tube into a can lying sideways; or he can hit the ball through a tin can with both ends open. Have him hit the ball up a cardboard ramp into a large tin can; or he can hit the ball around an obstacle course of four small cans.

Bowling

Collect 10 one- or two-liter plastic soda bottles. When they are empty, set them up pyramid fashion. Have your child roll a large, bouncy ball at them and see how many he can knock over.

Frisbee

You can make a Frisbee from a plastic lid of a coffee can or frozen food container. Have your child decorate it with markers. He can:

■ throw Frisbees through a cardboard box with large windows cut out.
■ throw Frisbees through cut-out holes in an old sheet, hung on a clothesline.
■ throw Frisbees and try to knock over paper cups.
■ throw Frisbees and try to land on a designated spot—like the sidewalk.

Tennis, squash, racquetball

You can make a simple child-sized racquet from a wire coat hanger that is open from top to bottom. Stretch an old nylon stocking over it. Fasten the ends with a plastic bag tie and bend the hook part closed. Tape over the hook to make it safe.

Use the racquet with balloons, which move slowly and are easy for your child to hit.

A good, inexpensive toy to help your child develop the eye-hand coordination needed to hit a ball with a racquet or a bat is a wooden paddle with a rubber ball attached with elastic.

Baseball

▶ Make a bat for your child by rolling up several sheets of newspaper and securing them with tape. Your child can practice hitting a balloon with this lightweight bat. When he is ready for someone to pitch to him, make a ball out of crumpled aluminum foil.

▶ To give your child running practice, tear apart a cardboard carton and cut out three bases and a home plate. See how fast your child can run around to them, being sure to touch each one. Have him compete against himself by timing his efforts. Be sure to praise each run.

▶ To practice throwing, have your child play a BASEBALL TOSS GAME with empty juice cans and an aluminum foil ball. Paste the following labels on the cans: home run, triple, double, single. Have your child stand in a special spot and throw his ball into the cans to try to make runs.

▶ This is a good game to use to explain how the game of baseball is played. If you attend local games together or enjoy watching your favorite teams on TV, your child can learn the fundamentals of the game. Make a diagram of the field out of cardboard. Let your child run his fingers around the field and count the bases. Have him identify the different shapes—the diamond field, the square bases, the round ball.

▶ Talk about the uniform worn by players, from the caps to provide shade when they're in the field and hard hats to protect them from being hit by the ball when they're batting and running the bases to the spiked shoes they wear to help them run without slipping. Have your child identify the numbers on the uniforms; the younger child will see two "twos," while the older child will tell you it's 22.

▶ Read books together about baseball. Try The Perfect Pitch by Beman Lord; Here Comes the Strikeout by Leonard Kessler; and Baseball—a New True Book.

▶ Take your child to baseball games, too. A young child probably won't last through nine innings, so plan accordingly. But, even if he doesn't understand exactly what's going on, he'll enjoy the crowd, cheering, and eating hot dogs and popcorn!

Watching the Big Game

Earlier I said that you should share some of the adult programs you enjoy with your child. In our house, watching sports on TV—football in particular—is a sport in itself. We seem to do it at all hours of the day and night, almost 12 months a year. Janet Horowitz has some terrific ideas for sharing this experience with your child—and making it full of learning and fun.

▶ Before the game, read simple books about football. Try <u>Football for Me</u> by Lowell A. Dickmeyer; <u>Football Players Do Amazing Things</u> by Mel Cebulash; and <u>Run, Kick, and Pass</u> by Leonard Kessler.

▶ Explain the game as simply as possible so your child will begin to get an idea of what is going on. Don't expect him to understand the whole thing; many adults don't either. You can make a large football field diagram on a sheet of cardboard that your child can play with as you watch. He can have little plastic people run around it. *"There are two teams. They are wearing different colors. They play on a long field that looks like this. Each team tries to get the ball to the other team's end of the field."*

▶ Talk about the football players and what they wear. Ask your child why he thinks they wear helmets and who else wears similar helmets.

▶ Talk about the colored uniforms the players wear. See if your child can identify some of the numbers on the backs. Have your child use crayons with the team colors to make a picture on white paper.

▶ Help your child make a FOOTBALL T-SHIRT for you to wear while you watch the game. On a plain shirt, have your child use permanent magic markers or fabric crayons—that can be purchased in an art store—to write the names of your favorite teams, football scores, footballs, and any other object that he associates with the game. He will get a thrill every time you wear it to watch TV.

▶ Make a FOOTBALL SCOREBOARD for your child to help keep score. This can be used to help your child with simple addition and subtraction also. *You'll need:* two sheets of eight-by-ten inch cardboard, a hole puncher, bookbinding rings, and forty blank index cards. First, punch two holes at the top of each sheet of cardboard, large enough for your bookbinding rings and far apart enough for two cards to fit without touching. Then, write the numbers 0-9 on the cards four times, so you have four sets of ten cards. Punch holes in them so they fit on the cardboard. Attach each set with the rings. Flip the cards back and forth as you keep score for each team.

▶ Let your child sit on your lap for at least part of the game. Channel some of your excitement and enthusiasm into squeezes and hugs.

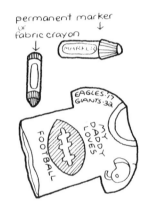

permanent marker
or
fabric crayon

TOGETHER

Make a football beanbag to toss back and forth during the commercials. Use the beanbag to play the Football Toss Game.

FOOTBALL BEANBAG TOSS

YOU'LL NEED:

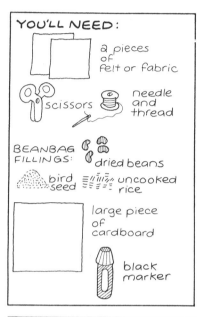

- 2 pieces of felt or fabric
- scissors
- needle and thread
- BEANBAG FILLINGS: dried beans
- bird seed
- uncooked rice
- large piece of cardboard
- black marker

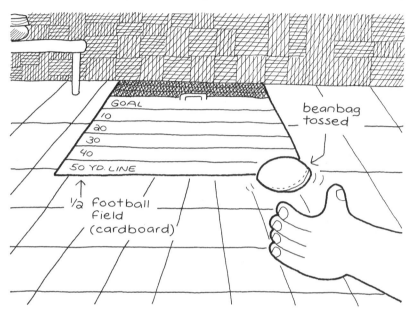

GOAL
10
20
30
40
50 YD. LINE

beanbag tossed

↑ ½ football field (cardboard)

WHAT TO DO:

1. Cut 2 football shapes from felt or fabric.

2. Fill with dried beans, rice, or even bird seed. Sew closed.

3. Reproduce ½ of the football field on piece of cardboard.

4. Stand back and toss the beanbag football onto the field.

5. GOAL: to toss the football beanbag onto the goal line.

6. Try standing different distances away when you play.

SPECIAL OCCASIONS 10

Celebrate! Celebrate!

Partytime

Before the party

During the party

The party ends

Family gatherings

Before the visit

The visit

A new baby

Celebrate! Celebrate!

The last nine chapters have been about the everyday chores and routines you experience with your child. This last chapter is about those special times that come up during your day and during the year that are celebrations.

One of our most important jobs as parents is to teach our children how to celebrate both the large and small things in life—traditional holidays, special achievements, the first orange leaf in the fall, or the rainbow on a rainy day. Some children have a hard time dealing with the excitement, disrupted routine, and the increased attention that can result from a special occasion. With careful and sensitive planning, you can create a supportive and relaxed atmosphere for your child in the midst of the festivites that will help him enjoy himself fully.

Big celebrations and holidays are exciting—sometimes too exciting for your child. Weeks, even months, before the actual event, he is stimulated by TV ads, store displays, and talk about plans. Whether it's Christmas, Passover, or a family wedding, it's important to remember that the needs of your child don't change just because there's a special occasion coming up.

Your child's routines should remain as close to normal as possible. Missed naps, late meals, or a rushed story at bedtime can ruin the fun and excitement for him—and for you, if he becomes fussy and difficult. Keeping to regular schedules will help your child feel secure amid all the new people and experiences.

During busy holidays, provide quiet times to discuss any questions your child might have about what is going on. These times will be harder for you to schedule, but it's more important than ever to keep in touch with your child's feelings and to let him know you are there for him, if he needs you.

Invariably, big celebrations bring special foods—many of which are rich, sweet, and spicy. Your child's menu should be kept as simple as possible. Serve nutritious foods, party-style, and try to limit his intake of sugar and snack foods. These can make your child irritable and just plain sick to his stomach and spoil everyone's good time.

Try to plan your child's participation in the celebration around those times in the day when he is most relaxed and receptive to new experiences. Just before naptime or bedtime, it is NOT a good idea to introduce a host of unfamiliar relatives or an exciting activity. Many young children do not enjoy or belong at adult dinner parties. Let him help pass hors d'oeuvres and talk with the company. Schedule dinner after your child has gone to bed. Remember to allow time for your child to prepare for and recover from special events.

With a preschool child who is making daily learning advances and discoveries about the world around him, each day is a new celebration. Learning to tie his shoes; ride a tricycle and then, taking turns on it; losing a tooth; all of these are special events that deserve some kind of recognition. Never overlook an opportunity to make your child feel good about himself.

You can recognize these events and accomplishments with a card or just a big smiling face in the mailbox or under his plate or pillow that says *"Great! You buttoned your sweater all by yourself"* or *"Wow! You really worked hard helping Daddy weed the garden. It looks terrific."*

Encourage your child to think of something special to say or do for someone else—a friend, teacher, relative, or maybe the nice clerk at the grocery store or the mail carrier. Help him write a special note of thanks to someone: *"Dear Ms. Hayes, Thank you for helping me pick out the book about Clifford last week. I really like it. Mom and Dad read it with me every night."* Have your child dictate and illustrate the note.

Celebrate the "little" things that happen every day which you enjoy. Have a picnic on the day you see the first buds appear on the trees. Make a snowman after the first snow. Read a book about frogs when you see the first tadpoles in the pond. Do something special on the longest and shortest days of the year. Your child will come up with lots of suggestions once you get started.

And, that's the point. Finding so many things to celebrate in his daily life helps your child get through those times when nothing seems to be going right. Big celebrations and little ones—there's always something to be glad for.

Partytime

Birthdays are special occasions that we all get to celebrate once a year. Your child's birthday is a special event that should be just for him. Let him help you in the planning and preparation. This is important for several reasons: first, it is a terrific learning experience for him; also, knowing what's going to happen will make him feel more secure and relaxed when the time comes, and last, but not least, the emphasis of the party will stay where it belongs— on him, the people he likes, and the activities he enjoys. So many times, parents get caught in the trap of trying to plan a party they think their child will enjoy, one that's bigger and better than little Amy's was last month. What you might enjoy and what impresses the other parents may very well not be your child's idea of a terrific party.

Here are some tips from veteran preschool partygiver, Janet Horowitz, to make your child's party fun and enriching for all.

Before the party

▶ **GUESTS** Check with your child. Try to invite the same number of guests as your child's age plus one. (Invite four guests to a three–year–old's party.)

▶ **INVITATIONS** Mail or hand deliver them, so there is no mix-up about date, place, or time of the party. If you're planning to serve lunch or dinner, mention it on the invitation.

▶ **PLACE** Inside, confine the party to one area of the house. Move as much furniture as possible to the sides of the room to get the largest space possible. Young children need lots of space to have a good time. If you're planning the party outside, be sure to have indoor plans (or a rain date) in case of bad weather.

▶ **PLANNING** Let your child help as much as possible. Some children know exactly what they want. For example, they might want a pizza party, a trip to the zoo, or a magician. If the budget is an important consideration or you wish to have it in your home, state this before you ask for suggestions. Let your child choose what he wants to do, within limits you have set. Consult Great Parties for Young Children by Cheryl Barron and Cathy Scherzer; How to Give a Party by Jean and Paul Frame; The Party Book by Bernice Wells Carlson; The Golden Happy Birthday Book by Barbara Shook Hazen; and Confetti by Phyllis and Noel Fiarotta for ideas. With your child read Happy Birthday to Me by Anne and Harlow Rockwell, about typical birthday preparations.

▶ **DECORATIONS** It's not really important to a young child whether or not you have a theme unless your child has a particular interest; so you don't need the expensive paper products. It's more fun if you make your own. Balloons and streamers seem to be the most popular. Attach balloons to everything, including the walls, using static electricity. Let your child create some decorations, too. For a festive looking table, a colorful paper napkin on a white plate works well. Have each party guest decorate his own styrofoam cup with magic markers.

During the party

▶ While you're waiting for all the guests to arrive, let the children get acquainted with the party room. Set out some simple toys to play with. Set up a doll corner and, in another area, have small plastic cars and blocks or wooden clothespins to make roads. If the party is outside, borrow some riding toys so there will be one for each child. Only put out toys your child is willing to share. It's not fair to expect him to be a good host if someone is clutching his special favorite teddy.

Remember that while young children love each other's company, they will play more with toys than with children. That's why games sound like fun, but may be hard to get going at a preschool party.

Activities

▶ Make PERSONALIZED HEADBAND HATS. Before the party, cut one strip of oaktag or thick paper for each guest and write his name on it. When the guests have all arrived, sit the children in a circle with magic markers, gummed stars and strips, crayons, sparkles, colored paper, wallpaper samples, paint samples, safety scissors, and glue in the center. Let the children decorate their headbands. When they have finished, staple one end to the other to fit each child, and let them wear their hats during the party. The headband serves as a nametag and a favor!

▶ Give each child a T-SHIRT and a supply of permanent magic markers. Let them draw a picture on the shirt. Then, write each child's name on the back of the shirt. Children can wear them home as favors.

▶ Have a peanut or lollipop hunt. Hide these before your guests arrive. Give each child a small bag to collect the treats and take them home at the end of a party.

Games

Over the years, certain games have become traditional at parties. If you plan to have several games, intermix the active and quiet ones. Be sure to play a quiet game right before you eat. Forget prizes with young children. They play just for the fun of it. Unless everyone can win, prizes can take away from the enjoyment of the experience. When explaining the rules of a game to young children, you'll have better luck showing them than telling them. You might practice beforehand with your own child so he can help you demonstrate. Don't worry if they never get the rules straight. As long as everyone is having a good time, it doesn't matter how the game is played. Here are some old favorites to get you started:

■ "Pin the Tail on the Donkey" You can also pin the nose on the clown, the tail on the bunny—a cotton ball—the mouth on Raggedy Ann or Andy, or the hat on the cowboy.

■ "Musical Chairs" Instead of chairs, try using stepping stones (pieces of construction paper or cardboard) that the children must step on. "Pass the Shoe" (teddybear or balloon) is another variation of this game.

■ "Follow the Leader"

■ "Duck, Duck, Goose"

■ "Hokey Pokey"

■ "I See . . ." The children have to guess what you're describing.

■ "Red Light/Green Light"

■ "Simon Says"

■ "Apple Bobbing" in a tub of water or trying to eat a donut, marshmallow, or cookie suspended from a string.

If you've forgotten the rules to any of these games, you can get complete directions to these and others in: Games for Children by Marguerite Kohl and Frederica Young; Games (And How to Play Them) by Anne Rockwell; New Games to Play by Juel Krisvory.

▶ Don't forget to sing with the children. They love it! It's a great way to wind down from an active game before you eat or before the children go home. Try any of the old favorites: "Twinkle, Twinkle, Little Star"; "Row, Row, Row Your Boat"; "Mary Had a Little Lamb."

Refreshments

Your child will probably be most concerned about his cake and its decorations. He will know exactly what he wants so let him help you make the final decision on what to serve. Let him help you bake the cake or choose one at the bakery.

▶ As an alternative to the traditional birthday cake, the children might enjoy decorating their own cupcakes. Set out a few kinds of frostings, raisins, M&Ms, sprinkles, gumdrops, and coconut. Give each child a plain cupcake and let him create a masterpiece.

▶ Sweet treats are standard fare at parties but you may wish to serve healthier foods to your child and his guests. Try an APPLE FROM OUTER SPACE by giving each child an apple, some pretzel sticks, and small cheese cubes. The children poke holes in the apples with forks and then, stick a pretzel in each hole. Last, a cheese cube goes on each pretzel stick. Part of the treat comes in making them. Older preschoolers might enjoy constructing RACERS with celery sticks or green pepper wedges, filled with cream cheese or peanut butter as bodies, and cucumber slices or cherry tomatoes or radishes as wheels (held together by toothpicks). Have a little car show.

The party ends

▶ Have the children sit in a circle and open the presents. If you do this at the end of the party, each guest will get to see his gift opened and appreciated, but things won't be destroyed before your child has a chance to enjoy them.

▶ When everyone has left, try to spend some quiet time with your child talking about the party. Before bed, read Benjamin's 365 Birthdays by Judi Barrett. Ask your child if he would like to have a birthday every day.

CAKE 'N ICE CREAM

YOU'LL NEED:

 1 angel food or other type tube shaped cake
 1 pint ice cream
 1 package instant vanilla pudding
 ¼ cup confectionary sugar
 1 cup cold milk
1 regular size container Cool Whip
 mixer and bowl
spoon
knife (ADULT USE ONLY)

WHAT TO DO:

1. Adult cuts off top ¼ of cake (Save cake top for later.)

2. Cut a well in cake, leaving ½" all around. Scoop out cake with a spoon.

3. Fill well in cake with ice cream.

ice cream

4. Replace top on cake.

5. MAKE FROSTING:
(a) Mix pudding, cold milk, and sugar. Beat 1 minute. Let set for 2 minutes.
(b) Fold in Cool Whip

6. Frost cake and place in freezer.

Frosting

Family Gatherings

Big celebrations and holidays invariably bring families together. This can be fun and exciting or scary and boring for your child. These gatherings are times for adults to renew acquaintances and reminisce, but meeting lots of people, many of them for the first time, can be intimidating for the young family member. It's easy to forget that the people you have known and loved all your life are often strangers to your child. As always, a little planning and preparation will pave the way to a more relaxed and festive time for all.

Again, according to veteran partygiver and partygoer, Janet Horowitz, there are three keys to successful family gatherings involving young children.
■ Get your child involved and excited about the gathering.
■ Help him get to know and feel closer to his relatives and your friends.
■ During the party, keep him interested, busy, and happy, so that you can be relaxed and have a good time.

Before the visit

First, get your child involved and excited about the family visit. Talk about how grandparents are Mom and Dad's parents and aunts and uncles are parents' sisters and brothers. Tell stories about when you were your child's age. *"I used to play house with my big sister, who is your aunt Robin."* Bring out any pictures you have. Young children don't completely accept the idea that adults were once little and your child won't really understand the family connections for a few years; but, he will love hearing the family stories.

If people from far away are coming to visit or you are going to their house, your child might like to speak with them on the telephone before the big day. Perhaps, they can send your child a short letter or postcard, just to get acquainted.

Tell your child exactly who will be at the party. Suggest that your child make a small surprise gift for each guest. This might be a special picture for each person to hide under their plate at the table or a little plant he has grown in a styrofoam cup—decorated by your child with his name on it—for seeds or cuttings. These must be started at least a month in advance; make more than you need, in case some do not grow. Try bean seeds, apple seeds, grapefruit and orange seeds, right from the fruit; also unpopped popcorn.

If you are going to another home, be sure to take along your **Travel Activity Kit** (page 130). These are distractions for your child once you arrive, also.

On the way, you might want to talk about things you'd like to find out about different family members. Once you arrive and at the dinner table, your child can "interview" his relatives about their hobbies, favorite things—ice cream flavor, season of the year, color—sports, and family memories. Remind him to give others a chance to ask questions, too, and that it's okay if someone doesn't want to answer a question.

The visit

Your child is not going to be able to sit through a three-hour dinner listening to adults chat and smiling politely. As long as he is quiet, well-behaved, and seems content, just cross your fingers and do nothing. Include him in the conversation, whenever possible, and have other distractions on hand for when he gets (justifiably) bored.

If the group is informal, they might not mind your child quietly playing at the table with some of the small toys, puzzles, and games you've brought in the **Travel Activity Kit**. In many families, it's better for him to be excused in between courses to play on the floor or in the next room.

If it's in your home or you've planned well in advance, you can hide peanuts in their shells around the house beforehand. Have him find the hidden nuts and put them in a special dish on the table. When he can't find any more, he can count them and shell them for everyone to eat. (When he counts the number of people at the table and gives them each a peanut, it's one-to-one correspondence!)

After dinner, if the group are game players, your child can participate in some simple charades or other games, discussed in Chapter 8. This might be a good time to take out some old family photo albums and look at the pictures together. Of course, point out everyone who is at the party, but also, take this opportunity to ask some learning questions.

- ◼ *"How many children are in this picture?"*
- ◼ *"Who is the tallest person? The shortest?"*
- ◼ *"What game is Uncle Tory playing?"*
- ◼ *"How do you think Uncle Dave is feeling in this picture? Happy or sad?"*

Let your child tell you everything he can about what is going on in the pictures. By drawing inferences about the people and events, he is practicing important thinking skills.

If your child likes doing artwork, provide him with a large sheet of paper, paste, scissors, and old magazines and suggest that he make a family collage. Based on all he has learned about family members, he can go through the magazines and cut out pictures that remind him of his relatives — what they like to do, play, eat, or music they enjoy. He can glue them on the sheet of paper and then dictate the names for you to write.

Take pictures of everyone, so that, after the gathering, you and your child can make a book to remember the special event. After everyone has left or you have gone home, have your child recall the details of the visit—who was there, what you had to eat, and what games you played. Bring this book out next year, or the next time you plan a family celebration, and your child will look forward to the day with eager anticipation.

A New Baby

Well, you've almost finished the book; and hopefully, the suggestions have steered you and your child to many rich and rewarding experiences. If it has helped you organize your time with your young child and made life more enjoyable and rewarding for the whole family, then this last special occasion may be the result of your success. It is natural for a new family member to arrive, as your preschooler is solidly on the road to becoming that happy, healthy, independent individual I have been discussing all along.

A new baby will bring many changes to your family, especially to her big brother or sister. You want the baby's arrival to be a positive, memorable experience for your child. With some preparation, time, and effort on your part, it will be.

▶ Don't jump the gun and tell your child about the coming event too soon. Unless he has been listening to others and asks you what's going on, don't discuss it with him until two or three months before the due date.

▶ Check some books out of the library to help you explain the physical side of things. A Child Is Born by Lennart Nilsson is an excellent book to help your child understand about the development of the fetus. Making Babies by Sara Bonnett Stein, a book with special information for parents and children, is another good resource. Everett Anderson's Nine Month Long by Lucille Clifton explores the emotional side of your child's wait.

▶ When you are preparing for the new baby's arrival—getting her furniture ready, mending and washing baby clothes, buying supplies—do something special for your first child, as well. Let him help you; but, also get him his own baby doll with miniature nursery equipment. Dress his doll in his old baby clothes so he gets used to the idea of someone else wearing them. Have him help you choose which of his old toys the new baby might like. Respect his need NOT to share one or two special things.

▶ Your child may think that the new baby will be a playmate right away. Show him pictures of when he was a baby. If possible, visit a friend who has an infant to avoid disappointments. Read That New Baby again by Sara Bonnett Stein and I Love My Baby Sister (Most of the Time) by Elaine Edelman to explore these feelings and expectations.

▶ Have a shower for your child. Invite a few friends; gifts might include things that he can use to help you take care of the baby, matching T-shirts, and toys that both children will enjoy.

▶ Make a special T-SHIRT for your child to wear, as soon as the baby is born. You'll need: a T-shirt, fabric crayons, paper, and an iron. Let your child draw a picture of himself doing something "grown-up" on the paper with the crayons. You write "I'm a Big Brother (Sister)" on the paper backwards. Follow the directions on the crayon box and iron the design into the front of the T-shirt. This can turn jealousy into pride every time he wears it.

▶ Before leaving for the hospital, you should tape-record some of your child's favorite stories and songs, also some loving messages. You may want to write a few notes beforehand to be delivered to your child while you're away. In most situations, siblings are invited to visit the hospital, but if this is not possible, have someone take an instant developing picture of Mom and the new baby to reassure your child.

▶ Encourage your child to choose one of his old toys to wrap as a gift and give to the new baby. The baby might "bring" him a gift from the hospital, too.

▶ When the baby arrives, give your first child a bunch of lollipops with pink or blue ribbons to hand out to his friends and well-wishers who drop by.

▶ Ask your child to help you with the birth announcements. He can lick the stamps or seal the envelopes; these activities will help him feel more a part of what is going on around him.

▶ Your firstborn will be experiencing many different feelings toward the new baby and you. Reading books about other children and their feelings may help him to express his emotions. Try That New Baby by Patricia Reif; She Come Bringing Me That Little Baby Girl by Eloise Greenfield; A Baby Sister for Frances by Russell Hoban; The Baby by Jon Birmingham.

▶ Take lots of pictures of your children together. They are both growing and developing and it's important to recognize and appreciate all the changes. Put them in a scrapbook and have your older child dictate a caption for each one.

▶ PUT THIS BOOK AWAY IN A SAFE PLACE. YOU'LL NEED IT AGAIN IN A FEW YEARS!